# NOTHING TO LOSE, EVERYTHING TO GAIN

## HOW I WENT FROM GANG MEMBER TO MULTIMILLIONAIRE ENTREPRENEUR

## RYAN BLAIR
### WITH
## DON YAEGER

PORTFOLIO / PENGUIN

PORTFOLIO/PENGUIN
Published by the Penguin Group
Penguin Group (USA) Inc., 375 Hudson Street,
New York, New York 10014, USA

USA | Canada | UK | Ireland | Australia | New Zealand | India | South Africa | China
Penguin Books Ltd, Registered Offices: 80 Strand, London WC2R 0RL, England
For more information about the Penguin Group visit penguin.com

First published by Nothing to Lose Publishing 2010
Published in different form by Portfolio / Penguin, a member of Penguin Group (USA) Inc. 2011
This paperback edition with a new foreword and chapter published 2013

THE LIBRARY OF CONGRESS HAS CATALOGED THE HARDCOVER EDITION AS FOLLOWS:
Blair, Ryan.
Nothing to lose, everything to gain : how I went from gang member to multimillionaire entrepreneur /
Ryan Blair.
p.   cm.
Includes index.
ISBN 978-1-59184-403-7 (hc.)
ISBN 978-1-59184-599-7 (pbk.)
1. New business enterprises.   2. Strategic planning.   3. Entrepreneurship.   I. Title.
HD62.5.B553 2011
658.1'1—dc22
2011004053

Printed in the United States of America
1   3   5   7   9   10   8   6   4   2

Set in Minion Pro
Designed by Vicky Hartman

PORTFOLIO / PENGUIN

**NOTHING TO LOSE, EVERYTHING TO GAIN**

Ryan Blair is a self-made multimillionaire and serial entrepreneur. He established his first company, 24/7 Tech, when he was twenty-one years old and has since created and actively invested in multiple start-ups. As the CEO of ViSalus, Blair turned the company around during the 2009 recession and, in three years, took it from $600,000 in monthly sales to over $600 million in annual sales. He lives in Detroit, Michigan, with his son, Reagan.

To my mother, Erla Hunt,

you gave me life, love,

and strength. I will always work hard to make you proud.

# AUTHOR'S NOTE

Since *Nothing to Lose* was published in August of 2011, a lot has changed. At that time, I was hoping my mother would miraculously survive her fall down a flight of stairs, which caused severe brain injuries and put her in a coma; now, eighteen months later, we have hope that she will make a full recovery. At that time, I saw my son's autism as an insurmountable obstacle for him and a very difficult thing for me as a father; now the prognosis is still the same, but we've made significant progress toward teaching him that his disadvantage will become his advantage. At that time, my company, ViSalus, had gone from near failure to doing roughly $20 million a month in sales, and I had a deal to cash out on ViSalus that would have paid me over $50 million; now I've set up ViSalus so I could run it for the rest of my life and build the company into a force to end the worldwide obesity epidemic.

In the following pages, you will find the details of the aforementioned journey and my perspective as a result of being part of one of the greatest successes in business. I've updated the content to reflect my new perspective, and I've added a bonus chapter about how to deal with the naysayers, the people who don't believe in you on your entrepreneurial journey; it's called "Told U So," specifically written for my haters. I've also added a page to my Web site where teachers and students can find educational resources based on the information in this book; please have a look: www.nothingtolose.com/resources.

# CONTENTS

# FOREWORD

by Nick Sarnicola

Ryan Blair is the most frustrating human being I have ever met. He is complicated, he is emotional, he changes his mind, he distorts reality—he is a mystery to me. Yet in spite of all his idiosyncrasies, he has taught me more than anyone else on Earth has.

Ryan Blair is also the most inspiring human being I have ever met. He is brilliant and charismatic, he is passionate, he is an open book, he is easy to forgive. And because of this he has taught me more than anyone else on Earth has.

This is the enigma that is Ryan Blair.

As one of the founders of ViSalus, the company Ryan is CEO of, I've had the opportunity to experience this enigma on a daily basis. As Ryan's (soul) brother, best friend, and business partner for the last decade, I can assure you that he is all of this and more. There are few people, if any, that know him as well as I do, which means few people will have the great pleasure to learn from his accomplishments and failures in such a unique and personal way as I have. My wish for all of you is that in reading *Nothing to Lose* you can experience even a fraction of him as he bares his soul on paper.

And baring his soul is what he does in this book. "Showing his thorns" has always been important to Ryan. He has a core belief that if he hides nothing and shares his deepest, darkest secrets, people will respect him, learn from him, and love him for it. And they do.

As opposed to just another business book where someone writes about all of the nice, fluffy moments in their career, making you wonder how they stayed so "perfect" the whole time—and leaving you feeling insecure about how hard business (and life) has been on you—*Nothing to Lose* teaches you how to handle the good, the bad, and the ugly.

Entrepreneurship is hard. Life is hard. But, if you surround yourself with the right people, the right business partners, the right books to read, and the right mentors to learn from, then you just might find yourself on the other side of money and filled with joy at the same time. Let this book be one of those books. Let Ryan be one of those mentors.

I remember the first time I met Ryan. It wasn't one of those moments where I felt like, "Wow, I'll be working with this person for a long time." In fact, it was quite the opposite. Ryan was on the brink of selling his company SkyPipeline, and Rich Pala, a mutual friend and business associate, sat us down for lunch in Camarillo, California. The dialogue we were supposed to have quickly turned into a monologue by Ryan, and one hour later I was asking myself, "Did I even say anything?" That was the only contact I had with Ryan for many months.

The second time I met Ryan, he had just sold his company and had been living the life of a playboy with no regrets. I walked in, tail between my legs as the leader of a failing network marketing company, trying to raise capital to recreate it, ready for the rich golden boy who had just sold his company to dominate the conversation again with an air of "Told U So" about him. Instead I found a humbled MAN—humbled by the harsh reality that the money he had worked so hard for was nearly gone because of the ignorant purchases of a twenty-six-year-old with more money than wisdom—journal and pen in hand, full of questions about me and my business model, and ready to get to work with a heart full of passion.

This is when I fell in love with Ryan Blair. I realized that this was a man who could change, who could grow, who could lead others—because he had led himself. This was the man I wanted to follow. This was the man I wanted to run the company that Blake Mallen and I had cofounded. This was the visionary ViSalus CEO sitting across from me.

I would be lying to if I told you the relationship has been a breeze ever since. But what long-term relationship is? We have fought like brothers, disagreed like business partners, yelled like best friends, and cried with each other like an old married couple. We have seen success, and then failure, and success again, and more seemingly insurmountable failure. We have bet it all and won. We have gone "all-in" on several occasions and barely lived to tell about it. Behind it all was always the irrational wisdom of the kid off the street, the kid who beat the system, the kid who became a world leader on entrepreneurship, the man who wrote *Nothing to Lose* to inspire millions of others to live their dreams.

I will be forever grateful to Ryan for teaching me entrepreneurship. I now lead tens of thousands of people without blinking an eye because he gave me confidence. He gave me a standard to follow and eventually I became that standard. Then came the day where I took everything I learned from Ryan and told him, "Follow me."

In the next section of this book, "Read This First," you'll read that our company was on its way out of business in the wake of the 2008–09 financial crisis. Our model was broken, and people were quitting. Customers and leaders left by the thousands and everyone blamed us, including our investors. As my ViSalus cofounders and I each put our last million into making payroll, I knew intuitively that something drastic would have to happen to right the ship and save the company.

That's when I stepped up. As Ryan had taught me, I acted like I had nothing to lose.

Days later I sent an e-mail to my cofounders explaining everything that was wrong with the company and why it wasn't working. I held back nothing and let the punches fly. My e-mail was my resignation as the Chief Sales Officer of ViSalus. My mentor Ryan Blair always taught me "Don't bring me a problem without a solution," so I brought a solution: I was going to fire Ryan as my corporate boss and sign up as an Independent Promoter of the 90-Day Challenge that we had just launched and show the world my own version of "Told U So." From the field, I would prove the business model and Ryan would focus on the corporate side, and working hand in hand, three years later we are on the verge of being a billion-dollar brand.

This is the greatest testament of Ryan Blair's wisdom documented in *Nothing to Lose*. He taught me entrepreneurship, he gave me confidence, and as only the GREATEST teachers do, he eventually let me become the teacher.

And that is why I thank God for the enigma that is Ryan Blair.

@NickSarnicola, cofounder of ViSalus

# NOTHING TO LOSE,
# EVERYTHING TO GAIN

# READ THIS FIRST

Los Angeles is a city that's famous for a sign. The ultimate symbol of my neighborhood is the white lettering you can see nestled in the hills between the buildings as you drive through Hollywood. Like the city where I live, the defining symbol of my life is also made up of letters, the letters *L* and *A* overlapped like the Dodgers logo, but where the *A* crosses over the *L* there is an AK-47.

I live in a penthouse apartment in an exclusive building in Hollywood where each night when the local clubs let out, a steady flow of celebrities spills over into the complex for after-hours parties. Anyone from billionaire Paul Allen to Jessica Biel has stopped by my spot, and accordingly, my crib is decorated to reflect my lifestyle. I have a pool table instead of a couch. And I have a collection of rare art and literary works I've acquired over the years. One of the unique pieces is a painting with the LA/AK-47 design, which I commissioned fashion designer Bryden Lando to paint for me, based on one of his most popular T-shirts.

It symbolizes the violence I grew up with, and it reminds me of the times when I actually used to carry around an AK-47. It was my most valuable asset back when I was a troubled young gang member—it protected me in the LA riots and in gang shootings. Now the painting on my wall could buy a truckful of those guns.

Next to this painting is a locked glass bookcase full of books, first-edition books by Napoleon Hill, Dale Carnegie, and several others from friends such as Jerry Rice, Bode Miller, Coach Dale Brown, the late John Wooden, and one special title that was given to me by Bob Goergen, a world-renowned entrepreneur and investor, when he bought my company. Inside the cover of the book reads an inscription: "Welcome to the Blyth family. We look forward to a profitable future together, Bob Goergen 8/08."

From the outside it looks as if I have this great, easy lifestyle. The truth is I've never made a million dollars easily, and I've made many millions of dollars.

It was August 2008, the same date as the inscription on the book, and I was on the ultimate high. I'd just sold ViSalus in a deal that, coupled with a multiyear earn out, was pegged at $120 million (or more if we performed greater than expectations) to a public company called Blyth, owned by the Goergen family. I celebrated my victory on the Donny Deutsch show, Fox News, MSNBC, and all over the wires. E-mails of congratulations from Wall Street to Main Street flooded my in-box. I had done something no one had ever done in my industry: we negotiated ten times our forward projected earnings in 2008 and eight times our earnings over the next three years. Never has a company as small as ours in the direct selling industry been bought for as large a valuation as we'd gotten. In essence, we'd received something better than what we'd have gotten if we'd taken the company public. As I was walking on set to my Donny Deutsch appearance, I received a text from my girlfriend at the time, who was also on set; she was a model on NBC's *Deal or No Deal*. The text simply said, "You're going to be a father."

Almost immediately after I came to grips with the fact that I would be a father (fatherhood is a serious thing to me, given that my biological father was a deadbeat), the U.S. economy went into a death spiral. A few short months, by December 2008, the president's economic adviser announced that the American economy had fallen into a "depression." The announcement was paired with a report from the U.S. Department of Labor that more than 533,000 Americans had lost their jobs in November 2008, and 1.9 million Americans had become unemployed during that calendar year. And I had a first-born child on the way.

As a student of entrepreneurship I knew this was a rare moment in history. Having studied capitalism and the impact of the Great Depression I knew that sixteen of today's Dow 30 companies were founded during a recession or depression. Corporate icons like General Electric, Johnson & Johnson, Procter & Gamble, and Disney were formed when times were tough. I started writing this book to rally the pioneering spirit in Americans and I called it *Nothing to Lose* after the mind-set I used to climb out of poverty and become a multimillionaire CEO.

Fast-forward to December 2009. At this point, ViSalus, the company I had just sold in a deal valued at $120 million, was worthless. Sales had dropped from $2.5 million a month to $600,000 over the year. That profitable future Bob Goergen had inscribed in my book was anything but. Blyth had lost faith in my business and written it off. The recession had exposed flaws in our business model—flaws that our overconsuming target customers didn't pay much attention to when they'd had access to credit cards and home equity lines, the value of their homes was appreciating, and their incomes were on the rise.

In good times, weak businesses prosper. And it turned out that I had built a business based on good times. Blyth had paid me a premium for a company that was now worthless to them. All the executives who had fought to pay me the ten times valuation that I had so vehemently negotiated in 2008 had egg on their faces. The people who were against the deal were proved right. And I was the poster boy for the guy who took a public company for a lot of money.

That December I was summoned to Blyth headquarters for a special meeting in the same boardroom I'd sat in to negotiate the terms of the sale of ViSalus the year before. I was asked to come alone. But they did send out a suit from Greenwich, Connecticut, headquarters to Los

Angeles (who claimed to know more about my business because of his MBA), to babysit me while I prepared a presentation they wanted me to give at the meeting, so it would be up to their corporate standards.

As it stood, I had put nearly a million dollars of my own money into the business to try to revive it. I'd voluntarily agreed to a $1 a year salary the minute the economy went south. I had a newborn son to think about, and it worried me that I might have just bet his future as well as my own on a business that was about to die. The company needed at least a million more to get through the next few months, but that probably wasn't enough—and I knew it. I might need $2 million, maybe $3 million, and at this point we had put $26 million into it. What I needed more than money was a beacon of hope. I needed my investors to look at me and say, We know you're going to make it, Ryan. We believe in you as an entrepreneur; we are on board with your vision.

It was a winter day in Greenwich. I put on my Sunday best and walked into that meeting. It was clear within seconds that nobody wanted to hear my presentation; they wanted to crucify me. They had investor's remorse. One by one they tore into me, until one of the managers got so angry at me that he stood up—biting his tongue, red in the face—and walked out of the room.

I remember feeling like I was back in my gang days, when the older gang members would try to punk me because I was a kid. I said in my head, *You better have respect. I'm not a kid.*

They told me in no uncertain terms that they wouldn't support ViSalus. They'd written it off. They wouldn't participate in this round of funding. They hammered the last nail into the coffin as hard as they could and told me not to let the door hit me on the way out. And rightfully so. I deserved it.

I flew back to LA and was immediately infected with the swine flu, and spent the entire Christmas holiday in bed. I asked myself over and over whether I should quit and jump ship. I'd argue with my ego that it wasn't worth my time, and my ego was doing a lot of talking. I'd wake up at all hours of the night, angry at myself. Why did I let that MBA suit influence my presentation? I was mad at myself for borrowing money for the business. Spending millions on fair-weather friends and fast times. I should have predicted what had happened to the economy. A CEO has nobody to blame but himself—and I knew it. It was my fault and I wasn't going down like that.

I had nothing to lose, and I was going to show my investors, and the rest of the world for that matter, that I would fight my way out of the corner.

I spent Christmas Day alternately throwing up and making phone calls, rallying employees, friends, family, the two other founders, Todd Goergen, and some other investors—and most important, myself. In the end, we came up with the million dollars, but it was for a business that had deteriorated so much that not even I had hope for it. Todd sent me an e-mail saying he had faith in me, that this time next year we'd be giving each other high fives. I dismissed it. I've never had to have an investor motivate me.

And that's when another blow came. I received a letter from my partner Nick Sarnicola and my vice president of sales, Mike Craig, that they were resigning. The letter was just like the manifesto from the movie *Jerry Maguire*. It listed all the things that we needed to change. I started reading their five-page rant and I couldn't finish it. I actually received it ten minutes before I was to hear that the board was moving to replace me. I was livid.

I'll never forget pacing around the hotel room where I received the news that I was losing two of the most talented people on my staff, and that I would be fired by my board of directors. (I knew this because friends in the industry had told me.)

After my anger subsided, I was overcome with exhaustion. I gave in and got on my knees to pray. I couldn't take it anymore. I had to ask for guidance to get through the most difficult business situation I had ever been in.

Clear in my mind and in my heart, I went back to Nick's letter, then called him up and said, "Let's do all the things on your list." We agreed to move him and Mike to entrepreneurial roles in the sales field and to put everything we had behind them to lead us out of the recession.

Once that strategy started to come together, I knew, even sitting in meeting after meeting, faced with the ultimate criticism, that I knew better than they did. I knew, whether they backed me or not, that I could turn the ship around. I thought to myself, *I know our customers better than these guys do. I'm the entrepreneur here.* During our October 2008 Vitality event in Las Vegas, the Goergens had stood up in front of a thousand or more of our distributors and boasted that one day ViSalus would be the strongest, most valuable company in their holding. And even though that statement seemed so far away in 2009, there was a bit of a masochistic streak in me that was still excited to try to prove them right. For some reason I felt alive knowing that I had no choice but to win.

So in the end I went with my gut instincts. We started redesigning our business around a new economy, a new consumer, and around the move of two of my most talented sales executives to the field. And it turned out that the plan I'd tried to outline in the presentation I gave that day in 2009 was the winning strategy.

Today, ViSalus is far more valuable than what Blyth paid for it. The company went from $600,000 a month in sales in December 2009 to over $600 million in sales for all of 2012. Based on our current growth, by the time you read this, that number will be far more. My meetings in that boardroom at Blyth headquarters are completely different now. So I got the vindication I wanted. And what did I really have to lose if I had been wrong? Actually, a lot: my business, millions of dollars, and my son's future, not to mention the embarrassment of being a failure.

But the reason I have a company today that's worth far more than it ever was is that, despite the circumstances, I played as if I had nothing to lose.

It reminds me of the speech Steve Jobs gave at Stanford in 2005. He said that "in the face of death, all fear of failure and embarrassment disappears."

I've faced the reality of death; I've faced the flash of a muzzle, the loss of my father, gang murders, friends who committed suicide—a failed business is nothing compared to that. When you have that level of survival instinct in you, it is your greatest asset. Like that AK-47 used to be. And that's why that painting hangs on my wall. So I'll never forget where I come from and what it took to get here. It hasn't been easy. There have been obstacles to overcome every step of the way, and a lot of looking in the mirror and fixing things that were broken. This book is not a self-help guide to a better life; this book is the road map I used to overcome adversity I've encountered. By sharing it, I hope you, too, can create your own road map to success in life and business.

# 1

## WHERE I'M FROM

--------

I didn't start out at the bottom—but I reached it quickly.

Long before I became a millionaire entrepreneur, I was a kid with a criminal record, street gang experience, and a lot of emotional scarring from years of abuse from my father. My teenage years were hardly the typical starting point for a normal, productive life, let alone a successful business career. Turns out, that didn't matter.

The first decade or so of my life was actually unremarkable in a pleasant, upper-middle-class kind of way. My family lived in a small, comfortable community in Southern California. No one was exceptionally wealthy where we lived; but just a town or two away were the billionaires' hot spots, and a town or two in the other direction was the ghetto. We knew where we were situated on the ladder, and we were all pretty content there.

My family had a pool, lots of nice clothes, and at Christmas, a new bike or scooter if I wanted one—we were doing pretty well, by most people's standards. And then, just as I was hitting my middle-school years, my dad got hooked on drugs.

He'd always had a pretty intense personality. My five older siblings had already learned to watch out for his temper; as the baby of the family, I had learned that lesson almost as soon as I learned to walk. But he wasn't a bad guy.

That's the thing that always gets me. When people hear my story now, they say to me, "Your dad sounds like a terrible person." He was terrible to live with once his life really started falling apart. But he wasn't a terrible person—not at first, anyway. In fact, I learned a lot from him.

For example, when I was a kid, I was rewarded through compensation. If I got a base hit playing baseball, there would be a certain prize at the end of it, like a new batting glove. I was always competing for something. It was my dad who offered these rewards—he was the first person to instill in me a work ethic and a risk-reward mentality.

He didn't believe in allowances; he believed in chores, and he paid me to do them. If I washed the cars, I got $5 per car. If I mowed the lawn, I got paid for that, too. Maybe it's not the best arrangement for every family, but it certainly worked for me. I came to associate effort with profit.

But it was more than just profit. Dad taught me about the pride that comes with hard work, too. He would always give me recognition among his friends and coworkers as he told them what a strong worker I was and how much I earned; as a result, I would try to work more and more. He bragged to one of his friends about my paper routes and I loved making him and his friends proud, so soon I had three paper routes.

I also learned how to get the most out of an opportunity to make money. My dad paid me a dollar per bag of weeds I pulled from the yard. If I could persuade the neighborhood kids to do it for fifty cents, then I could turn a profit by having several kids fill a number of bags at once, while I worked on another paying chore. Thanks to my father, it was instilled in me early on to have ambition, motivation, and appreciation for money.

But the psychological impact of his poor upbringing, his insecurities—all his issues—ended up getting the best of him. That's what ultimately pushes everyone who goes in that direction, isn't it? His "issues" pushed him into drugs, and everything else spiraled out of control.

My dad was middle class, but he lived as if he were among the elite.

He leveraged himself as so many Americans do—financed his cars, borrowed to buy his house, spent his last dollars on making our house look pretty—to make himself feel more important. He lived beyond his means and started using drugs to cope with it all; that was his undoing.

One afternoon I was playing in the backyard with friends and my dad came home to my surprise. He had a look of shame on his face unlike I'd ever seen. Dad had lost his job. I found out later from my mom it's because he'd been caught doing meth in the bathroom, and the execs of the company where he was the vice president at had finally gotten wind of it and set up a sting operation to catch him.

That was the end of my father's career and the beginning of him becoming a career drug addict. At the time, there were three children still at home—my older siblings had already moved out. As if my dad's failure gave them the excuse they were looking for, their lives seemed to fall apart as well. They all left home, one by one, until I was left alone with just my mother and father. One sister moved in with a druggie boyfriend; another ran away and lived on the streets for a while. Finally, when it was just my parents and me, the bottom really fell out of my life.

My dad used to love showing off his gun collection, and I did too. One time, a few days after I had shown them to my friends, the older brother of my best friend broke into the house and stole every last gun. I didn't find out until several years later who had actually been involved, but at the time, it didn't matter. Dad thought I'd done it.

By this time, the meth was making him paranoid and even more violent. He swore I'd stolen them and sold them, and he threatened to kill me if I didn't give them back. After all I'd seen, I knew that I didn't want to stick around for the repercussions. It was dangerous. That night I called my sister Stephanie and told her, "It's real. Dad is promising to kill me if I don't return the guns, and I have no idea who has them or where they are. Save me."

As grateful as I was for my sister's offer for me to stay with her, the new situation presented its own set of challenges. She was living with a musician at the time. He might have been an aspiring rock star—there are a lot of those in Southern California—but he certainly didn't have rock star money. They were living in a tiny, dirty house and surviving on macaroni and cheese, which was all either one could seem to afford.

When I arrived at their house, they walked a sleeping bag out to a dilapidated little shed in the back, tossed it in, and said, "Here you go." It was a shack. It had doors, it had a window, and it had holes in the walls. There's no nicer way to describe it. But I was away from my dad, and at that moment, that was the most important thing.

A few days later, I went to a thrift store for rolls of carpet that people would donate after they redecorated their houses. There were a couple of pieces that were large enough to serve as insulation, so I pinned them over the walls to try to block out some of the weather. It was Southern California—not the most extreme climate—but it got cold at night, so I ran pieces of carpet over the doors to try to keep out the wind. I did have a tiny space heater, though, and the electricity to run it, and that helped me make it through the winter.

But the weather was not my biggest enemy. That distinction belonged to the lice that infested the shack.

It didn't matter how much I showered or what I tried to do to my hair to get rid of them—the next day they would be back. I could feel them crawling down my head and onto my back while I slept on the floor on the beat-up mattress that eventually replaced the sleeping bag. Finally, in an act of desperation to be rid of the lice, I decided to shave my head. Michael Jordan's dome gave shaved heads a big boost in the '90s, but the look hadn't really come on the scene yet. Shaved heads were definitely not cool at that time. The first time I showed up to class bald, the school bully walked up to me, slapped me in the back of the head and said, "Ryan Blair has no hair." It became the favorite taunt at school, in an annoying, singsongy cadence that poked every nerve in my body, even as I tried to ignore it.

I lived in that miserable little shack for close to a year. I felt that I couldn't go home as long as my father was there and still an addict, and my mother clearly wasn't planning on leaving him anytime soon. So I stayed at Stephanie's, feeling that even though I was the one who'd left, I'd been abandoned by both of them.

Finally, when the principal of my school, Dr. Judy Dunlap, called me into her office to talk to me about my failing grades, I spilled it all: the issues with my parents, the shack I was living in—I told her everything. Suddenly, my grades were the last thing on her mind. "We have to call social services. We have no choice," she explained. "What you are telling me is that you are in danger."

By law, the principal also had to get me to a psychologist, and she demanded that my mother go along, too. After I recounted to the shrink everything that had gone wrong with my family over the past few years, he looked my mom in the eye and said, "You are the abuser."

My mother was shocked. "It's his father!" she insisted. "He's the bastard! He's the beater and he beats me, too."

The psychologist just shook his head and told her, "You're a grown adult, and you are letting your child go through this. You are negligent by law, and we are going to take him away if you don't make things right immediately. You have no choice but to act right now."

This made my mother reevaluate the situation for the first time because, in her mind, she was the victim, not me. And she *was* a victim. She took the punches that I never got because she had stepped in front of my father. I remember her face being black-and-blue and her telling people she'd been in a car accident. I remember watching him throw the punches, and I remember him dragging me into the room to have me watch—as a warning that I should never stand up to him. I remember once seeing him point a gun to my mother's head and telling her he was going to kill her if she didn't quit crying. There is no question that my mother was a victim. But in her mind, she had endured all of the abuse so that I wouldn't have to. It never occurred to her that I was being damaged anyway.

She finally agreed with the psychologist that she had to take action, so she called my father that night and told him, "They are going to put Ryan in foster care, so you need to leave. I'm bringing Ryan back to the house because he's living in unfit conditions, and they are going to inspect us here."

That was what broke her from him—that the state was going to intervene. She took a stand, and we hoped it meant turning a corner for everyone. But after about three months, my father started dropping by again and was as violent as ever, coming after both my mother and me. Whenever the attacks would start, I'd run out of the house and back to my sister's, which still seemed like a better option.

My mother was determined to protect me this time, though. She found a little one-bedroom place next door to my sister and somehow managed to scrape together the $500 deposit without my dad's knowledge. One day she told me to pack my belongings, so I piled into the car all of the things that matter most to a thirteen-year-old: my Nintendo, my CDs, and my clothes—all the trappings of my family's pleasant, middle-class life that, in the end, were just part of the sham.

We moved everything over to the new house and then went back to the old house for one last carload of my mother's belongings. By the time we returned, our new place had been gutted. Everything inside was gone. Someone had watched us carrying in boxes, waited for us to leave, and then had broken in and taken it all.

My mom was hysterical. Here she was going out on a limb in a last, desperate effort to break away from our abusive situation, and we were robbed blind on the first day. The police weren't able to help us very much, either. The officer who arrived in response to our call advised us not to file a report. We lived right next to a park where all the vagrants and gangsters hung out. We saw scary-looking men congregating there, some with teardrop tattoos by their eyes and prison tattoos all over their arms.

They watched us coming and going—inspecting us in a way that made my skin crawl. "If I take a report from you," the officer told us, "they are going to know you told on them, and they're going to get revenge. I'd suggest for everyone's safety that you just let it go."

My mother was crying from the sheer helplessness she felt at that point. The officer reached into his pocket, handed my mother a twenty-dollar bill, and said, "I'm really sorry this happened to you." Then he turned to me and said, "Hey, son, you do not want to tangle with those guys. Do not get mixed up with them, whatever you do."

And that was the welcome we received to our new life.

## WELCOME TO POVERTY

Dad eventually found out where we were, but I guess he figured he was better off without us; he never made an effort at that point to get clean. Because my mother had taken me away to try to protect me, walking away seemed like a good idea to him, too. He disappeared from my life for the next fourteen or fifteen years.

Mom and I both tried to make the best of the situation. She got a job at the deli in a local supermarket and tried to break free from her own drinking problem; I would play basketball at the park to try to keep out of trouble. I didn't do a very good job, though—trouble was all around me, and I figured it was easier to join in than to fight it. Whenever I'd be out shooting baskets, guys would approach me and ask my gang affiliation. I told them I didn't have one—the whole idea of street gangs was still pretty new to me.

But I quickly saw how the system worked, how the street lords kept themselves in power through influence and manipulation. I observed how the older people used bribery and fear to get the younger kids to do their crimes, and I saw how the young people willingly went along with it because it seemed like the only power structure that had any kind of respect in the neighborhood.

It was a flashy, angry, tempting world of getting what you want and not caring about the risks. The risks were part of the esteem—the more brazen your crime, the more respect you got. As a scrawny kid who felt powerless against everything going on in my life, that appealed to me. I don't blame anyone or anything else but myself for my choices. But I do understand how a competitive, hyperactive, and confused person could easily allow himself to get caught up in it all.

My behavior and grades plummeted again. This time, I was an eighth grader, and I got kicked out of school. Two months into ninth grade, I was asked to leave high school, too. I wasn't big—my growth spurt was still a year or two away—but I was mouthy and always arguing with the teachers to the point where they felt threatened.

Every day I came to class with a chip on my shoulder, thinking, *None of you could ever understand what I'm going through, so how dare you tell me what to do? It's interesting when you tell me that one day algebra is going to be important to me. Do you understand that in my life right now, my survival is what's important to me? And you're telling me it's really important that I listen to history? I'm going to go home and get jumped on my way back or have a gun pointed in my face, and I'm supposed to care about what you have to say?*

The teachers immediately diagnosed me as a problem kid. They fought to get me Ritalin for ADD and Prozac for depression; they fought to get me out of the classroom. That was fine with me. It was easier to hang out on the streets, anyway. Breaking into cars to steal stereo equipment and resell it was easier than working for what I wanted, so I figured that was a better route for me.

I landed in juvenile detention a couple of times, which actually ended up being a positive thing in the long run, because it was there that I discovered my fascination with computers, which in turn led to the development of my first company many years down the road.

The other positive thing in my life during that period was Randy Pentis. He was a local cop with the type of face only a cop could have—all hard lines and ill humor. When I was a teenager, the sight of this face meant only one thing: the certainty of unavoidable punishment. One glimpse of this man would send my gang scattering down the street like billiard balls in a break, ducking behind buildings and flying around corners. I was desperate to get away from the police officer who had made it his personal agenda to keep me from making the mistakes I was determined to make.

I remember Sergeant Pentis best for the grip of his hand on the back of my shirt, and for the time he dragged me up the walkway in the middle of the night to wake my mother and explain to her why her son wore the bandana, the sneakers, the belt, and the rest of the gang attire. Randy Pentis is the man who arrested me—more than once. And he challenged me to do better for myself than I was doing at that time. But the results of that lesson were years down the road, too. At that moment, I was an out-of-control teenager who seemed destined for prison.

Then my mom started dating a man named Robert Hunt.

## YOU'RE NOT MY FATHER

Over a few years, my mother had moved up from making minimum wage as a deli clerk to being the department manager, and she met Robert when he came to the store as a customer. He was a successful, stable businessman who owned his own real estate company. I'll never forget the day I first met Robert Hunt. One day I saw a Cadillac Allante pull up onto our dirt road. A man was coming to pick my mother up for a date. I thought, *Who is this bald-headed guy coming to see my mother?*

I was extremely protective of my mother, and when I shook his hand, I braced myself for confrontation. But I couldn't find any sign of bad intention in him. By all physical appearances I had nothing to worry about. He was short and pretty skinny. And he had this sense of humor that wore down my defenses.

My mom asked if I would come to dinner with them at his home. The last thing I wanted to do, as a soon-to-be-eighteen-year-old man, was spend time with my mother and her boyfriend. Bob could sense I was reluctant for more reasons than one, though. I had an issue with the idea of having a man around my mother and me.

He said, "Tell you what, you drive."

I looked over at his Cadillac and I thought about it. It might be fun. I'd never driven that kind of car before.

"But there are only two seats," I said, looking for an excuse to not have to join them for dinner.

Bob said, "I'll get in the trunk."

Bob wasn't a man to take an excuse from anyone. Certainly not from a punk seventeen-year-old kid. I thought, *I'd like to see this happen.*

True to his word, Bob climbed into his trunk and I closed it on him; then I got into the driver's side of the car and sat down. My mother sat in the front seat, and Bob peeked his head through a hole in the back seat and began to navigate me all the way to his home. I remember thinking that with my track record, if we got pulled over, having a rich man in the trunk might not go over well.

They hadn't been dating very long when Robert invited my mother and me to move into his house. He made the offer after being absolutely horrified by where we lived. My mother was a little hesitant, but Robert explained that it would get me away from the crowd I'd been running with, out of the bad neighborhood where we were living, and it would give him a chance to have a more direct influence over my life. He knew that at the rate I was going, getting out was the only shot we had at success. My mother and I realized that we had nothing to lose.

I was seventeen years old when the move happened, and Robert insisted that I live with him and my mother until I was at least eighteen. I agreed to the arrangement because I didn't really have an alternative. But I didn't fit in on Westlake Island. For one, I had gang tattoos all over me, because when you fight for a living, the more wounds and ink you have, the less you have to fight.

I'll never forget the day I pulled up to the gates of Robert's beautiful, upscale neighborhood in my '78 Toyota Corolla station wagon. One of the security guards recognized me; his name was Terry, and he ran one of the few legitimate businesses in my old neighborhood. We'd bring him our recyclables to weigh, then he'd give us a voucher for the supermarket.

"What the hell are you doing here?" Terry grumbled at me as I slowed my car. I told him I lived there now. "Get the hell out of here! You don't live here," he said.

I grinned, assured him that I really did live there, and then added, "You work for me now." He laughed. As he waved me through the gate, I realized just how much my entire life had changed.

Looking around me, I started to observe how people lived—not when they were burglarizing cars for a living, and not when they were only pretending to have a lot of disposable income, but how people who were legitimately wealthy lived. I realized that it all came down to the work they put into themselves and their professions. I realized they had a system, too. A system of wealth that was unlike the system that ran the streets.

One time I was driving my stepdad's car to get it washed, and an older gentleman approached me and asked casually, "So what do you do?" I guess he thought I was a celebrity or an athlete to have a car like that as a teenager. And with that experience, and others that followed, I got to observe how society attaches labels to you. I started wearing polo shirts and dressing nicely. Girls at school were suddenly allowed to date me, whereas before I'd been off-limits to most of the "nice" girls. No one seemed to know, or care, that he hadn't raised me from birth. I acted like the son of Robert Hunt, a very successful real estate entrepreneur, and I worked for him.

To me, that really was what mattered—the idea that I worked for him— that even as a teenager I was a professional. Reaching back to my childhood, before the gangs and the violence and the drugs, I found the work ethic my father had instilled in me, and I dusted it off.

My first job with Robert was running errands and doing general chores around the office. After a while, he gave me other tasks, the main one being the service of eviction notices on families who weren't paying their rent (three-day notices ordering tenants to pay rent or quit the property) and foreclosure notices.

For some people, throwing families out of their houses might seem kind of harsh, but I saw things differently.

People were falling behind on their payments either because they'd gotten into properties greater than what they could afford or because they'd made bad spending decisions and chose to fund the illusion of prosperity rather than meet their real-life obligations. And it wasn't just some faceless corporation that got stuck paying for their mistakes, it was Robert—my mentor. When someone didn't pay the rent for three months, that deficit didn't just disappear. It came out of Robert's pocket. So, in essence, each delinquent tenant was passively robbing him.

I took my job seriously. I wanted every family to have a fair chance to get caught up on their payments or to find a new place to live, so I made sure I delivered every notice promptly and respectfully. Many people got their affairs in order and nothing further came of it. Others simply refused to leave, and at that point, my job was to make them move.

During this time, I was eighteen years old, six foot three, and weighed 240 pounds; and I'd spent a lot of time in rough company. I never used physical force with my job. Robert wouldn't have tolerated that. I did cut an imposing figure, though, and I wanted to prove myself not only to my stepdad, but also to myself. Each time I'd pull up to a house, I'd brace myself for a confrontation. People talk about the significance of sweat equity when they were first starting out. I know a thing or two about it—I had literal sweat equity trickling down my back and dripping down my forehead, making my eyes sting.

Robert Hunt, my stepdad, he was a stickler, but he taught me so much that it wasn't long before my hard work paid off and I left his company because I got offered a job. The company was called Logix, and I started out as a customer service representative answering about 120 inbound telephone calls a day. Starting salaries were $6 per hour, and we'd get a small bonus every time we saved an account or got someone to upgrade. In that call center I learned a lot. I saw the turnover, the hirings and firings, and the training process. I saw a system.

Logix had a data center in the same building that was designed to support its call center downstairs. I'd always wanted to work there because I loved computers, so one day I asked if I could cover a swing shift for the data center. The experience was a chance for me to bond with the manager of the group, and he offered to transfer me from the call center to the data center.

I made the switch, got a raise to $6.50 per hour, and learned how to change the backup tapes and reboot computers if they went down—just basic stuff. But I didn't see it as menial; I saw it as a tremendous opportunity to learn how the company worked on a number of different levels. I was like a sponge, reading every book on computer science I could find and immersing myself in the subject.

In the meantime, I also started going to the community college because Robert Hunt had a rule that if I lived underneath his roof, I had to complete high school, go to college, and get a job. I didn't want to work for him anymore because I wanted to venture out on my own into the field of computers, so I took it upon myself to learn every last thing I could from classes, books and articles, and from talking to experts.

Because of my ability to hustle and my nothing-to-lose attitude, I was soon the lead data-center technician. Next, I was made the supervisor of the center, and then I was made the manager. Finally, at the age of twenty and after only about two years with Logix, I was made a vice president. I went from making $6 an hour to more than $100,000 a year. I will always be indebted to Keith Howington, the CEO of Logix, for giving me opportunity and mentorship at Logix. He taught me many lessons that I apply to this day.

But at that point, I realized that I could start my own company. All it took was a few indispensable ingredients: an idea, hard work, and dedication. Once I figured that out, I had no choice but to go to Keith and tell him I was going to start my own company. He wasn't too happy about that because he needed me to finish the development of a critical piece of software for a subsidiary we'd just acquired. And I couldn't care less about his happiness, because I was obsessed with my future as an entrepreneur. In the end he became my business partner, and we were both happy.

So what was the point of dedicating an entire chapter to explaining my life before I became an entrepreneur? There are several reasons.

First, I want to be honest. I don't have a sterling past. Chances are you're coming from your own set of damages and bad experiences. Use those to propel yourself to better things. Learn from them. If I can make it—starting out as a street kid and ending up as a stable citizen who enjoys financial success—anyone can.

Second, I had people who were willing to mentor me, to give me another chance, and to let me prove myself. Don't be too proud to accept help. That's going to be one of the most important aspects of growing your business, and you need to be okay with it early on.

Finally, I want to emphasize that we are not defined by our circumstances. Whatever situation you might find yourself in, it's easy to allow it to become the lens through which you define yourself. You are stronger than whatever circumstances you're facing. Remember that with the proper mind-set, potential is the one power you always have, and the mind-set that propelled me forward came from having nothing to lose.

# 2

## THE NOTHING-TO-LOSE MIND-SET

---

There is nothing more dangerous than someone with nothing to lose. Usually a series of losses will trigger it. You might have gotten laid off, or lost your home, or are going through a messy divorce. You may have started a business and failed. Maybe you've had to couch-surf for the first time since you were in your twenties. After a combination of events like these, one after the other, you realize one day that you're at the bottom.

This is where a nothing-to-lose mind-set comes from.

Like an animal backed into a corner, your survival instincts kick in. Now, there are two types of people. There is the type who will ignore his instincts and cower and submit. This is a domesticated person, and with enough pressure, he is the one who will take a route to a lesser existence, give up, or commit suicide. Then there is the type who, no matter how desperate the circumstances, obeys his instincts and fights. And just like that animal backed into the corner, there is nothing more dangerous.

I got arrested about ten times when I was younger. I only served time twice and, fortunately, I was never tried as an adult. When I went to

Juvenile Hall the first time, I was a skinny white kid, so I had to learn quickly about people with nothing to lose. The new guys always got tested to see how tough or domesticated they really were. What would happen if I bumped into him? Or better yet, what would happen if I walked over and asked him for his milk during lunch? Was he going to jump up and fight? Or was he going to hand it to me and say he didn't want it?

When you're in jail, it soon becomes obvious who is the real deal and who is not. And you know that if that kid lets you take his milk, he isn't as tough as he seems. Soon you'll be taking his milk every day. And so will everyone else.

The same principle applies to business. A lot of people come into my office with a front. They talk, and talk, and talk. And I test them. I start by asking for specific names, people they've worked with. Or I'll ask a business-model question that only the real deal would know. You had millions in sales, huh? So what was your cost of goods sold? What type of EBITDA (Earnings Before Interest, Taxes, Depreciation, and Amortization) did you have? Where'd you bank? Wells Fargo? So were you with the private bank at Wells Fargo? Who's your rep over there?

If the person can't answer these types of questions in detail, he is either a complete scam, or he wasn't the person actually responsible for the success of the business he's referencing. You'll find a business success has a thousand fathers, but I want to deal with the person who knows what it takes to win: the founding father, not the other 999.

When you're on the streets, you learn to read people for a living. You're always thinking, *Is this person going to stab me in the back? Rat me out? Set me up? Tell people where I live? Is my mother going to get hurt? Will I go to jail because of this person?*

When you've played the game with stakes as high as those, weeding out people who are fronting is instinctive. I didn't make up these behaviors—I know them for a fact because every situation I've survived and the many millions I've made came with a lot of stolen milk.

Now those street smarts and my nothing-to-lose mind-set are my greatest assets. And they can be yours, too. We'll be looking at assets in a later chapter, but if you've got your back in a corner and you choose to fight, that choice is going to work more to your advantage than anything else could.

First, you have to determine whether or not you're in a nothing-to-lose situation. Ask yourself, do you go to work every day afraid that you're going to lose your job? If you had to go into your boss's office right now and ask for a vacation, would you be able to do it? Are you dodging bill collectors? Do you live paycheck to paycheck? Do you feel as if you're sacrificing the best of your successes for someone else to take the credit?

At the coffeepot at work or at home around the dinner table, do you talk about how shitty your job is? If the answer is no, and you're happy— then congratulations. Maybe now isn't the right time to strike out on your own. But if the answer is yes, then there is no better time to stop thinking like an employee and start thinking like an entrepreneur.

Now, don't get me wrong, I don't hate employees. I'm actually an employee of the company I created, but the mind-set I have is that of an entrepreneur. And the biggest heroes in my company are the entrepreneurially minded employees. They treat the company as their own. You can also be an entrepreneur without any employees at all (I'm envious of you) as a consultant or with your own home-based business. But if you're going to get anything from this book, know first that the only thing you can't be is *just* an employee, that is, someone who is barely getting by every day, not pushing himself and not investing himself.

It's time to listen to those instincts and start fighting as if you have nothing to lose.

Some of you reading this are judging me and saying, Why should I listen to him when he's made bad decisions in his life? For those of you having a hard time getting over the fact that I haven't had a squeaky-clean life, I say take any middle-class kid whose family is in shambles— torn apart by drug addiction and abuse—throw him into a gang-infested neighborhood when all he wants is a male role model, and he will find males to follow but they won't be role models. That's why I've made bad decisions, but that's also how I got my nothing-to-lose mind-set. And those things you are judging—my poor decisions—those are my assets.

You can judge me all day long. You can judge my bank statements, you can judge the cars I drive, the art on my walls, and the homes I own. Like it or not, these are the rewards created by a person who had nothing to lose. And now I'll share with you how I went from having nothing to lose to having tens of millions to lose.

But a mind-set isn't enough; you're going to need to get smart—book smart and street smart—because there are going to be a lot of people trying to steal your milk. Read on.

# 3

# HUSTLERS, CHARLATANS, . . .
# AND TONY ROBBINS

---

In February 2010 I was invited by Stuart Johnson, the owner of *Success* magazine, to attend an event dedicated to Jim Rohn. Jim Rohn is considered one of the first people in the personal growth industry to take commonsense wisdom and successfully market it, and he was a man I greatly respected and admired. He'd just passed away, and all the best of the best were there to celebrate a retrospective of his work. The keynote speakers included Tony Robbins, Brian Tracy, Les Brown, Dr. Denis Waitley, and Mark Victor Hansen—men who have collectively sold probably about a billion books over the span of their careers.

There were around two thousand people in the audience, all excited to see these legends pay homage to the godfather of the industry. As I watched each one of these men get up there and try to give the greatest performance of their lives, I had an epiphany. It felt as if I were watching the end of an era. I thought, *This must have been what it was like when my parents saw the end of their parents' music.* You know how songs used to be all dreamy about good times and happy days, when musicians sang the music you wanted to hear, not the music their souls needed to release?

And honestly, this was my parents' music. My stepdad used to play Tony Robbins tapes, and go to fire-walking seminars. They believed that if you bought these books and listened to these messages, you would be a better person. Not to say there isn't truth in that statement, but we all know that what these motivational speakers were really selling was the façade of a perfect life, good times and happy days—a theatrical representation of life instead of the reality.

I kept asking myself, *Why do I have to listen to my parents' music? Why isn't Jay-Z up there? Where are the authentic people who will lead the next generation through the worst economic time since the Great Depression? Where's the rock 'n' roll of this generation?*

Our generation doesn't believe anyone has a perfect life. We think inspirational speakers are a joke. We want authenticity. Where are the leaders of our generation with the real stories to inspire us to greatness? I guess motivational speaking will always exist—there will always be a niche market for it—but it needs to evolve, and in the end, whatever is left standing will be authentic and what isn't will be gone, because our generation recognizes the smell of bullshit like no other. And frankly, most of the personal growth stuff that I read or hear is just that: BS.

On your journey, you're going to be compelled to invest in your education. You might listen to a motivational speaker, or buy a book, or listen to some audiobooks. I'm all for that, and I'll get further into it later in the book. But be wary because there are guys out there who prey on people just like you.

As a speaker myself, I entered the world of motivational speaking with an open mind. I had studied the Bible, eastern religions, and authors like Hill, Carnegie, and Nightingale, whose messages were absolutely pure. I came on the scene thinking that my colleagues were good people who cared only for the impact their messages would have on their audiences. I also assumed that the people doing the teaching were qualified to talk about their topics. Of course I found the opposite. Half the idiots out there pitching their seminars have never done anything but pitch their seminars.

I remember sitting backstage in greenrooms and hearing the most amazing conversations. One time a speaker walked offstage with a smirk and said, "I sucked the money out of the room."

Another guy asked him, "How much did you get?"

"Oh, two hundred fifty thousand."

You would think by the way they were speaking that there were twenty thousand people in the audience. Not at all. I've witnessed groups of no more than five hundred people part with more than half a million dollars in one sitting.

So what sort of value did these people get, in many cases, for having leveraged their lifetime savings and credit card balances? A recycled message plagiarized from every other hustler. A drug called "effortless prosperity." Another bit of wisdom I got from the greenroom—most junkies never open the box, one speaker told me.

The charlatans, gypsies, and snake oil salesmen of yesteryear still exist today. Only now they move from town to town under the pretext of "motivational speaker," "inspirational author," or simply "coach" or "consultant."

They claim to have captured prosperity like a genie in a bottle, and they'll grant you your wildest wishes—for a fee. *Buy my book and you'll be a millionaire in a minute! Buy my audiotapes and you'll be a billionaire! Enroll in my seminar and I'll teach you how to be a millionaire in two hours!*

So far in my life I've gone from fat to skinny and from poor to prosperous. Having made both journeys, I can tell you that there is no effortless strategy for either. I've had the chance to ask world-champion athletes, billionaire businessmen, award-winning actors, and platinum record–selling musicians about how they achieved success; and what I have found time and time again is the same response: the journey to the top of your chosen field is filled with effort and sacrifice, self-teaching, and total commitment.

Here's my advice while you're poking around this book looking for wisdom and inspiration. Understand that I'm not saying all motivational speakers are bad. I happen to despise the term because I don't think that the title "motivational speaker" signifies accomplishment. I've met many motivational speakers with whom you would not pay to trade places if you knew the truth about their prosperity. I believe there are a variety of messengers who will come into our lives with quality content. These messengers are not all bad, but you have to do your homework before buying from one. First and foremost, verify the credentials they have to teach you about their subject.

Remember, it's not just about past success, but also about present success. The shame is that most of these motivational speakers are out of touch with the times. Perhaps in the distant past they did something remarkable. Somewhere along their journey of life they decided to make a career out of talking about it as opposed to doing it. When you're really doing it and building wealth, you don't have time to give motivational speeches, unless of course there's something else to be gained from the speech than a measly stipend.

Unfortunately, the best messages of motivation and the best know-how for prosperity can only be found in taking action on a daily basis, fighting the competitive battle, so to speak. The people taking action are both students and teachers of the subject, something I've found to be a rarity in the industry of "motivational speaking." So-called "mentors" who offer up tidbits of advice for a fee are all hustlers, and it's not bad to be a hustler, but instead of buying a $10,000 weekend seminar on how to be successful, I'll give you all you need in ten steps.

1. Work your ass off.
2. Don't give up, ever.
3. When faced with defeat, rise to your feet!—Dr. Dre
4. Keep angling until you find your angle, then play your angle.
5. Sacrifice. (See chapter 11.)
6. You'll survive, no matter how bad it is—it isn't as bad it could be.
7. Shake off your mistakes, but try not to repeat them. (See chapter 12.)
8. Be grateful—most people don't even have a dream.

9. Remember that you are not safe. Even if you are on the right track, you will get run over if you just sit there.—Will Rogers
10. Go big, have fun. If not, you either quit, die unhappy, or have a midlife crisis and blow your success.

I know these aren't exactly the Ten Commandments, so in the next chapter I'll talk in greater depth about the philosophies I've used to build my businesses.

# 4

# PHILOSOPHIES FROM
# THE JAIL CELL TO THE BOARDROOM

---

**Y**ou don't have to be brilliant to be successful. I know plenty of people with less than three-digit intelligence who have eight-digit bank accounts.

But you do need to have solid philosophies and some kind of spirituality or enlightenment that will give you the foundation upon which you can build everything else, such as work ethic, integrity, and character. You also have to have rules by which you operate your business—the Golden Rules, I like to call them.

These are the principles that affect the way you think and the way you act and react. These aren't necessarily moral rules, though those are certainly important. The basic principles of business ethics are generally the same across the board. They don't vary much from business to business (though whether everyone operates by these universal standards is, unfortunately, another issue entirely). Your Golden Rules of business are a little different. They should be the ideas that shape your philosophies for management, sales, and networking, and for how you regard failure—and these are going to vary from person to person.

I'd like to share some of my Golden Rules so you can see that they are not really anything earthshaking but just a collection of quotes, concisely phrased ideas, and general reminders I keep close to me as I make decisions for my company. I've picked them up over the years, reading them in magazines or trade journals or hearing them from other people, and one or two I've come up with on my own. I just like how they capture various points.

I've divided them into five categories, depending on which area of my business they speak to: Communication and Management Rules, Business-Model Rules, Customer Rules, Strategy Rules, and Personal Rules. In short, they are rules to guide my thinking and help steer my decision making, and they are just as valuable to me as my business plan. These are the philosophies that work for me in any situation, from the jail cell to the boardroom.

## GOLDEN RULES

### Communication and Management Rules

*Life is theater; everyone is an actor—some in the lead, some in the supporting cast.*

This is an allegory I came up with one day while trying to describe the nature of teamwork. The lead often gets the attention and the accolades, but that does not mean that he or she is more important than the smaller roles that make the play possible. It simply means that each performance has a story that needs to be told and a certain number of characters who have a designated purpose within that story to help to tell it, move it forward, and get it to its conclusion.

The same is true in the business world. Everyone within a company shares a common goal: to create a superior product for the customer and, by doing so, earn a return for the shareholders. However, not everyone can be in the boardroom, nor can everyone be on the showroom floor or on the assembly line or making the sales pitch. It doesn't make any one role more or less important, because each is absolutely necessary to achieve the overall product. I think it's helpful to remember, too, that while the lead roles usually get more applause, they are also the ones who tend to get trashed by the critics!

*Never ask a question you don't already have the answer to.*

This lawyers' maxim is one that has an important place in business. Just as a lawyer does not want to be thrown a curveball in front of the court while examining a witness, a business owner does not want to be caught off guard in front of potential clients or investors. I can remember vividly when I broke this rule in a SkyPipeline board meeting. As the CEO of the company, I asked a question of the board, and I did not know the answer to it. Needless to say, I didn't like the response to my question. Afterward, my attorney, the late Joe Nida, pulled me aside and gave me this golden rule.

As a side note to this rule, though, I want to add another maxim: If you don't know the answer to something, say so.

*If you are unsure of the answer to a question, say, "I don't know, but I will get you the answer by [day, time, date]."*

I've seen countless executives in the boardroom (including some of my own, unfortunately) attempt to answer a question they didn't know the answer to, answer a different question, or evade the question altogether. If you don't have 100 percent accurate information or all the details in front of you, just say you don't know. I've made the mistake of guessing the answer to an important question, and it has often come back to bite me. One time I was asked where I expected a market to be a year later. I had no idea, but I gave an answer anyway, and my answer was way off. At the next board meeting, the same question came up again, and this time, my answer was totally different. The board noted it, and I noted that I would never answer a question I didn't have the answer to. You only have one chance to establish credibility. Don't blow it by attempting to have all the answers.

*"The secret of getting ahead is getting started. The secret of getting started is breaking down your complex overwhelming tasks into small manageable tasks, and then starting on the first one."*
—Mark Twain

Because I don't have an aptitude for thinking four or five moves ahead, I have to attack the first things first and worry about everything else down the road. That being said, this quote from Mark Twain offers some of the most valuable advice I have ever encountered. It seems simple enough, but it's often hard to remember when you're facing a mountain of seemingly impossible obstacles with your business. The key is not to view everything as one huge, looming project. Instead, focus on all of the individual elements that make up every bigger challenge, and then prioritize them.

Create a good old to-do list, and start working your way through it. If something seems too daunting to face at the moment, skip it if time and circumstances allow you to, and move on to the next item. When you get through your list, circle back to the beginning, and start with the projects you passed over the first time around. Each item you are able to check off creates a sense of accomplishment, which in turn creates momentum. But you have to be willing to take that first step, to tackle that first obstacle before you can hope to make any progress on the rest.

*When you feel you have failed at something, ask yourself:*

Why did this happen?
What could I have done differently?
How can I do it better next time?
What changes should I make in my strategies?
What can I do to improve my planning and preparation?

While it's important to move past our failures and not let them hold us back, it's equally important to make sure we learn from them so we don't repeat our mistakes. I really like the checklist above because it is fairly comprehensive in terms of evaluating the problem while focusing on the positive. It allows me to hold myself accountable without beating myself up. I call this process the postmortem, whereby we go back and evaluate our failures to make sure we learned our lessons so we don't repeat the failures.

I suggest keeping a notebook specifically for lessons you learn the hard way. Take the time to actually record the answer to each question so you have a written reminder of what went wrong and what you resolved to do differently. Share these questions with your employees, too. If your whole team is continuously focusing on improvement, failure will be a valuable tool for learning rather than a roadblock in the way of progress.

*Master taking action.*

To become a "master" of something, you must work with focus and purpose. That is my goal each time I set out on a new project or explore a new industry. I want to master it. I want to immerse myself in it so I can know everything I possibly can about it.

But that kind of dedication isn't limited to learning. I also strive to become a master of action—someone who is never content to sit by the sidelines but who is always engaged in the process of selling, networking, expanding, negotiating, researching, and exploring. In short, I want to be *doing.* I have resolved never to be content with simply watching my business; I want to be covered in its mud and grease and blood and sweat and tears. So if I go down, I'm going to be fighting when I do.

*Never express a negative emotion in an e-mail or text message.*

Under no circumstances should you communicate negative emotions via e-mail. These conversations should be had in person or over the phone. John Tolmie, the CFO of ViSalus, has what he calls the twenty-four-hour rule. If he feels he might respond emotionally to something going on in the business, he sleeps on it and responds the next day. This is outstanding advice for any business leader.

You can't control the conditions in which a person is reading your message or how he or she will react to it. What if that person is reading it during significant family stress or after just having lost a loved one—would you still send it? You never know what's going on with people on their end, so you can't know how they will interpret your words. Don't leave difficult communication to chance.

Don't forget that once something is written down, it becomes permanent. Do you really want someone to have a tangible reminder of when you flew off the handle? Always, always fight the urge to fire off an angry e-mail or text message. You will come across as more collected and professional, and you will not regret your decision.

*Praise in public and reprimand in private.*

You'll earn the love of your team when you praise them in public and single out individuals for a job well done; however, if you have something critical to say, I strongly suggest that you do it in private. Public embarrassment is a sure way to drive people to perform at a lower level. Imagine your fear if every time you made a mistake, you were embarrassed in front of your peers and colleagues—people whom you respect and admire. You would likely stop taking risks or putting in extra effort, and would probably perform only to satisfactory standards. The last thing you want as an entrepreneur is an employee who is only satisfactory.

Coach John Wooden lived by this rule, and so does former Louisiana State University basketball coach Dale Brown. Coach Brown once told me about the way he would inspire Shaquille O'Neal to perform at a higher level when Shaq was playing college ball. If Coach Brown observed Shaq underperforming, he would pull him aside and say, "When you played Kentucky, you dominated your opponent—he couldn't stop you, Shaq! This guy you are up against is not better than you. You need to play like you did against Kentucky. You are better than this. You are not playing like the Shaq I know!" But he would never, ever criticize Shaq's playing in front of anyone else.

To this day, Shaq credits Coach Brown's mentorship with much of his great success. If you don't learn how to convey disappointment effectively and if you criticize people publicly, you will eventually find that you've driven away your most talented people. But if you can motivate your team in the right way by celebrating accomplishments and quietly addressing shortcomings, you'll have their loyalty and respect.

## Business-Model Rules

1. You are a model-driven company. Test your assumptions, and revisit your model routinely. Rip the model apart every time you look at it.
2. Create a retention-based sales model; ideally, pay a long-term residual.
3. Know your customer.
4. Be as close to your customer as you can be.
5. Cherry-pick your new markets.

This combination of statements is a great one for any of my companies because it is full of action words like "test," "rip," and "create." It encourages each employee to get fired up about the product and the market, and it challenges everyone to be an energetic force in the growth of the business.

If you are not passionately engaged in the process, how will you ever really understand what it is that you're selling? I want employees who are willing to look critically at the product and who will offer suggestions. I want employees who are constantly looking for ways to improve our offerings and set higher goals. I want employees who care enough to invest themselves by taking an active role in our company's growth.

*Marketing exists to create sales.*

It sounds like a fairly self-evident statement, but sometimes it is easy to get wrapped around a promotion or an ad campaign because it is clever or catchy but not necessarily the best way to reach the consumer. Even in a campaign intended to build a brand image, the ultimate goal is to increase sales. The simplicity of this statement is a good reminder to me that marketing, as well as everything else within our company's structure, needs to be focused first and foremost on creating sales.

*The best formula for increasing sales:*
*Exposure × Conversion = Result*

Essentially, what this formula represents is the effectiveness of your marketing and of your sales force. Exposure is how you let people know about your product. Do you use direct mail? Viral marketing? Traditional media ads in print, radio, and television? Do you use social networking applications? How do you spread the word about what you have to offer, and how effective is each approach? This is what will determine your overall sales numbers.

The goal, of course, is to increase your rate of exposure while increasing the rate of conversion (i.e., how many people actually purchase the product). Methods of advertising do not yield equal results and can be dependent on any number of outside factors. Internet outreach, for example, can spread the word among young people but is not so effective in an older demographic. And while it can provide great exposure, it does not translate to a very high conversion rate. Direct mail usually only yields about a 2 percent conversion rate. From my experience, radio advertising has a conversion rate of about 0.5 percent, which is not bad, but it depends on which stations you select when determining whether you're able to reach the right demographic. Direct presentations consistently have the highest rate of conversion, but that rate is largely dependent on how skilled your presenter is and how compelling the reasons are to buy now as opposed to later. A good presenter can have a conversion rate of 85 percent; the challenge is that a direct sales presentation is not always an easy option to arrange for many products.

Whatever the case, this rule is an important one to remember. It is not advertising alone that will increase your sales. A strong and well-researched marketing plan is a crucial part of the formula as you seek to reach potential customers in a manner that is relevant and effective for the sake of making the conversion to sales and getting the results you desire.

*"It is not the strongest species that survive, nor the most intelligent, but the ones most responsive to change."*
*—Charles Darwin*

In jail the guy who rises to power is never the strongest or the smartest, he's the person who adapts to the ever-changing environment and influences the right people as prisoners come and go. Put plainly and simply, adaptation is key to survival. Keep abreast of market trends, and know when it is better to go with them and when it is better to radically depart from them. You need to be able—and willing—to change your game plan when conditions—such as demand, the market, or technology—shift. When PathConnect's business model looked like a failure, we realized that we had to shift our focus from white-label social networks to tools creation for brands that are sold directly to consumers. We took our company from a sure failure to a great return for investors in a matter of six months, because we adapted to our strongest competitive advantages. Darwin was absolutely right—in the wild world of the jungle (or of business), it really is survival of the most adaptive.

*Compensation drives behavior.*

Anytime I see a company struggling, I take a look at its compensation system. Almost inevitably, the rewards are not in place for hard work and aggressive, profitable sales strategies. Everyone in the company needs to feel connected to the company's success, either through profit sharing, recognition, or another type of compensation that motivates and honors dedication to the job and to the company's goals. In later chapters, we will discuss how to structure just such a plan for your company to take care of your employees and to bring out the best of their abilities for the benefit of everyone.

## Customer Rules

*Service is the greatest opportunity to differentiate.*

This statement is self-explanatory, but that doesn't make it any less important. I have found, time and time again, that the best way to separate your business from the pack is to provide customer service at a level that is unmatched by your competitors' services. If you put people instead of profit first, the difference will be apparent to everyone and will increase your sales and your customer loyalty better than any advertising or branding campaign you could imagine.

*Being people oriented is not an acquired skill.*

Related to the rule above, either you are people oriented or you're not. It's not something your business can "work on." You don't have time for that. It's something you have to have from the get-go and something you have to maintain consistently to build up the kind of reputation you want for your company. Make sure your employees understand this rule from the start; it's much easier to keep something great going than to try to rebuild yourself later to win customers back.

*"Don't fear your competitor; they'll never send you money. Fear your customer."—Jeff Bezos*

This rule from the founder, president, and CEO of Amazon.com is a profound piece of advice. Worry about your loyalty to your customer, not your customer's loyalty to you. This is an opposite approach to the common practice in which management spends time attempting to look through the customer's eyes back at the company. I prefer to ask these questions: How loyal are we being to our customers? What decisions are we making in the short term and long term that might make our customers feel we are disloyal? How do we treat them in our customer service group? If we outsource customer service, will they feel that we don't care about them? How are we giving more to our most valued customers—the ones who have been with us the longest, spent the most, and given the most feedback? These are the questions to focus on first. If you take care of your customers first, everything else will fall into place.

## Strategy Rules

*"An army everywhere is an army nowhere."—Sun Tzu*

Sun Tzu's masterwork is entitled *The Art of War,* but many of his lessons are no less applicable to the marketplace than they are to the battlefield. An army that is spread out widely may cover a lot of ground, but it loses its effectiveness and its potency because its force is too diluted. I learned this one because when I ran my gang I had to be careful if I started wars with too many rival gangs at once. I didn't want ten armies pointed back at my one.

The same is true of a company that tries to do too many things instead of concentrating its energy on developing one area in which to be superior to anything else out there.

A business needs to have a focus. I have found that without a clearly defined specialty (ViSalus is a weight-loss and weight-management company), it becomes harder and harder to develop a top-notch product because our vision and our resources are so scattered. This is, in essence, the "do one thing and do it well" philosophy.

*"One thing at a time, all things in succession. That which grows slowly endures."—J. G. Hubbard*

I love this quote because it reminds me that patience is the key. I might not see returns today or tomorrow, but with the right investment of time and effort, my work will flourish and last. Everything has a time and a place, and every process has a proper order. I can't rush something whose time hasn't come yet—that only creates instability. Instead, I need to remember that the things that develop over time are the ones that are more likely to reflect timeless ideals rather than brief trends or flash-in-the-pan popularity.

*"Keep your friends close, but keep your enemies closer."—Sun Tzu*

It is a sound philosophy. Abraham Lincoln lived by it. So does Bill Gates. Rather than allowing yourself to get sucked into a perpetual battle with your competitors, see if there isn't a way to bring them into the fold. Lincoln brought them into his executive cabinet. Gates gave them jobs at Microsoft. If there is someone out there with enough talent to pose a threat to your business, you might want to consider hiring him or her. After all, wouldn't you rather have that know-how and energy working for you than against you?

*"Most things wired will become wireless, and most things wireless will become wired."—Nicholas Negroponte*

In what has come to be known as the Negroponte Switch, Nicholas Negroponte, cofounder of the MIT Media Lab, made a startling and prophetic prediction that the technology industry would undergo a tremendous change as advances, functions, and needs developed.

When he first made this pronouncement, people thought it was absurd, but he was quickly proved correct. To me, this characterizes a man who was so intimately involved in the industry and so deeply ingrained in its inner workings that nothing escaped his notice, including inevitable (if seemingly unlikely) future trends.

*Drive your potential customers toward you with a compelling offer to take action now.*

You have to spark interest in your product offering. The first step toward making a sale is to reach out and attract attention. Create within your potential consumer a need to know. Try to get the potential customer to ask: Why is this product important for my life? Is it worth my time and money to learn more?

Of course it's better if customers are able to recognize right away how your product or service will be of value to them—and it's in this stage that you ultimately want to reach them anyway—so take the time to make your advantages and unique offerings clear, recognizable, and prominent. This can help propel the consumer to buy, often bypassing the need for further questions or a longer sales pitch.

## Personal Rules

*"Keep away from people who try to belittle your ambitions. Small people always try to do that, but the really great make you feel that you, too, are great."—Mark Twain*

More wisdom from Mark Twain—priceless. When I was first coming up, I had a lot of haters. Friends, family, and just about everyone who knew I was trying to be something would try to squash my ambitions. It would drive me crazy. And then I read the aforementioned quote given to me by Dr. Jerry Fecht, my professor of humanities at Moorepark Community College.

There will always be people who will hate on you and stand in the way as you try to pursue your goals. Whether it is from spite, ignorance, or jealousy, it doesn't matter. The fact is that you need to steer clear of people who are too shortsighted to recognize your potential—or too bitter to be willing to encourage it.

*"If you look for the bad in people, you shall surely find it."*
*—Abraham Lincoln*

This is another truism that Lincoln embodied, and I think it's applicable to what I believe about viewing the world, which necessarily affects how I run my companies.

I want my employees to have a positive outlook, and I want them to trust the customer. Any consumer knows when he or she is being treated with respect rather than contempt, suspicion, or apathy. The key to building and maintaining a loyal customer base is to treat customers in a way that demonstrates their value to the company. Listen to their concerns, be generous with your return policy or follow-up visits, and always keep their best interests at the heart of your business.

*"There is no finish line."—Bob Goergen*

If you are focused only on the day when the hard work ends, you'll never reach it. You're never finished; there's no end, only new races and new beginnings.

*"I'm not a businessman, I'm a business, man."—Jay-Z*

Spoken from a guy who, like me, came from nothing and took his entrepreneurial game to the next level. You are the business when you're the CEO of your own company. You're the brand, so you should build your brand as a business.

*I don't buy stocks, I make stocks.*

People often ask me what stocks I invest in, and because I take significant risk in the start-ups I'm affiliated with, I don't buy stocks in the stock market, unless I have the direct ability or control to build value for the stock. Stockbrokers need not call me.

*Honor your deals with God.*

I used to beg God to help me through the tough times during my youth, and he did. When I was in trouble and looking at some serious time, I made a deal with God that if he saved me, I would spend the rest of my life leading people to his kingdom and not my own. I said I would serve. He did save me and I have done my best to honor the deal I made in that jail cell. We all make deals with God. Honor them.

*Efforts don't pay the rent.*

When an employee tells me how hard he or she is trying, I usually respond with this thought. I deal in results, not efforts. Results pay the rent.

*You're either in control or out of control.*

I coined this quote when I was going through a tough time in a relationship. Then I applied it to business. Don't get me wrong, I'm not a control freak. Sometimes it feels good to put control in another person's hands, just not your bank account or your business.

*I make money; it doesn't make me.*

Own your relationship with money.

*It's a very bad idea to pursue too many good ideas.*

This is my mantra around ViSalus and all my companies. I get pitched about so many good ideas, but it would be a bad decision to chase them all. Make sure to be very selective in the projects you take on.

*"If you spend too much time polishing your image you'll tarnish your character."—Dale Brown,* Man in the Glass

I am the executive producer of Coach Brown's documentary and this is one of the most powerful quotes from the movie. I've been slammed in the media, I've been criticized by my friends, and I've been accused of everything from being a fraud to a drug dealer. My first instinct was to work on my image, but after I talked with Dale Brown about the subject, he told me to work on my character because it's the only thing I can control. People will give you a reputation; you give yourself character.

*"Throw dirt on me and grow a wildflower."—Lil Wayne*

When they throw dirt on you, they're going to see something they didn't expect. Adopt this belief system.

*"Go Pro!"—Coach John Wooden*

This is why I'm writing this book. Coach Wooden told me it was time to elevate my game to the professional level. He inscribed a book to me before he died; the inscription read "Dear Ryan, Go Pro!" When Coach passed on, I lost one of the few father figures I have ever known, and I plan to honor him by living my life at the professional level. RIP Coach Wooden.

*The only differences between you today and a year from now are the people you know and what you have learned.*

This has been one of the most important rules for my professional life. It reminds me to take advantage of every learning opportunity I possibly can. If I don't, I will never grow as a person or as a business leader.

It is each entrepreneur's responsibility to focus on development, maturity, perspective, and all the other things that go along with becoming a better manager and business owner. As another famous saying goes, "We cannot control what happens to us, but we can control how we respond to it." I believe this with every fiber of my being—what we make of our circumstances defines who we truly are.

Where will you be in one year? What will you have done with the opportunities put in your path? As the tattoo inscribed on my inner left bicep says, carpe diem.

# 5

## SEIZE THE DAY

---

There were a few times in my life when I saw into the future. One of the earliest examples is a vision I had from inside a jail cell about becoming a public speaker. I was reading the Bible out loud in solitary confinement and I had a vision of my doing that in front of thousands of people. Chills rushed over me and I knew right then and there that somehow I would do just that. It was as though God himself had given me confirmation. That dream came true when I was invited to speak at several churches in the Detroit, Michigan, area one very cold winter fifteen years after my jail cell premonition. The churches were filled with thousands of people and I addressed them from the same pulpit that Martin Luther King Jr., President Bill Clinton, President Barack Obama, and many others whom I admire have spoken from. The dream had come true.

We all have dreams, and confirmations like the one I received; we just don't listen to them. I did because all I had growing up were dreams. My reality was too terrible to think about. Dreams were my only hope in life, and so I learned to believe in them. I actually became a millionaire because I believed in a dream. I connected my dreams as one would connect dots. My dots are memories and dreams that I connect with faith.

The following dream is the one that made me a millionaire. It was my second major premonition, but the first that I would see come true. At this point I was twenty-one years old, living in the first house I owned, in Simi Valley, California. I'd raised venture capital and hired about thirty employees, I was in the media, and I'd earned my place among the who's who of the 40 Under 40 on the Pacific coast. To everyone, I was the whiz kid genius, stepson to the wealthy Mr. Robert Hunt, and a kid who was taking off. But inside it was a different story.

I remember nights when I'd lie in bed wide awake because I was afraid I wouldn't be able to make payroll the next day. I would get phone calls from my venture capitalist at all hours. One Sunday night I got a call from my lead investor and the chairman of my company, Fred Warren, telling me that I needed to fire my sales manager. Because I needed money from Fred to make payroll, I had to pick my battles wisely or lose everything. In this case I spent the rest of Sunday worrying about how I was going to fire my friend the next morning.

The war of internal dialogue would go on in my mind for hours— *I'm not going to do it. But Fred said I should do it, and he's right. And he's holding the company by the purse strings. I don't want to fire my friend. I'm not going to do it, f that guy. But am I not doing it because I'm afraid? If I can't man up and do this, then what can I do?*

After the most intense sleepless night of my life, I arrived at work and walked straight past all my employees as though I had something extremely important to attend to in my office, and shut the door. I sat there for hours, wondering how I was going to fire my friend. And then that voice came into my head, "It's either him or me." Finally, my fingers punched in my friend's four-digit extension.

"Michael, I need to see you."

By the time he got to my office after walking past his colleagues who had seen me walk in with an absolute intensity that morning, and the fact that he was the only person within the company I had asked to speak to, in combination with the expression that must have been on my tired face when he walked in, Michael had already put two and two to-gether. He immediately said, "You're firing me, aren't you?"

After a number of incidents like that, I had a dream that I'd sold SkyPipeline. I had designed the company to be sold and it was built to take advantage of a short-term gap in the broadband market, so it was on my mind a lot in those days. I was tossing and turning that night and I fell into a pseudosleep—one of those times when you have an intense dream, but you're fully awake.

In my dream I was being called into the boardroom of my attorney's office. It was a dark room filled with law books, and the walls were cov-ered in symbolic art of law and order. There they were, the members of my board, sitting around a big mahogany table. Titans and millionaires every one of them, private jet–flying world-renowned venture capitalists Fred Warren, Scot Jarvis, Bob Dilworth, Mark Ozur, Joe Nida, Glen Hartman, Jim Chow, and Rob Reagan. I looked around at the proud smirks on their faces. I felt completely in control. Someone reached out and poured a glass of fine red wine and handed it to me. A toast, they said, to the sale of SkyPipeline!

That was it. I'd arrived. I was a millionaire.

That dream was one of the clearest I'd ever had, and I remember it gave me chills all over my body. I woke up out of that sleep in a cold sweat and with the greatest clarity I had ever felt. I knew that dream would become a reality.

One day, not long after my vision, a competitor of mine made an offer directly to my board to buy SkyPipeline, and I did get called into my attorney's boardroom.

I remember I was nervous as I walked into that room, and there they were, my board members sitting around a big table, just like in my dream. But there was no celebration on their faces, no proud smirks. Their faces looked predatory—I could sense it. These people weren't my friends, wait-ing for me to arrive so they could make a toast to my genius. They were there for one thing—they were going to take me for my money. They wanted to steal my milk.

We'd had multiple bidders and we were about to accept one of them on their terms. I owned 20 percent of the company, and the offer on the table was $25 million. Everyone in the room was handed a piece of paper that stated how much they would get from the sale. I took one look at the amount on the sheet in my hands and looked up.

"There must be an error," I said.

"No," the attorney said. "This is the way the calculation worked out. You agreed to a five-times liquidation preference and antidilution provisions in the investor agreements."

I looked back down at the paper—the amount was zero. Thanks to these entrepreneurial vultures, I was officially in a nothing-to-lose situation.

I thought back to that dream I'd had while living my middle-class life, lying in bed in my middle-class home—a condo in Simi Valley that I'd leveraged to build my business. I thought about all the times I'd imagined the sale of my company and how I'd risked it all, but in the end of my dream my bet would pay off. This was looking more like a nightmare.

The board was silent. They were waiting to see my reaction. This was the moment they'd prepared for. They weren't playing checkers; this was real money, and they were five moves ahead of me at this point.

I must have turned a furious shade of red, because I could feel my heartbeat in my face. I sat there thinking, *I'm screwed! Who do these people think they are? After I worked twenty hours a day, sacrificed my friendships, lost my girlfriend, gained sixty pounds. I took their phone calls on Sunday nights. How dare they? They planned this.* And now I was supposed to vote their way, and walk off with zero. That's what they'd planned.

What they *hadn't* planned for, though, was what I did instead.

I told the board that I would sue every one of them, blow the deal, and sink the company before I'd walk away with nothing.

California law stated that they had to have my vote. And even though they were right, the contract I'd signed did add up to zero, I wouldn't do it. I was going to tell all the customers and employees about what they had done. I was going to call the CEO of the company that was going to buy us and tell him the deal is off. I'd tie this whole thing up in the courts forever. They weren't getting my vote.

Only two things motivate venture capitalists: fear and greed. When I walked into that boardroom that day they were full of greed, but when I left, they were full of fear.

A day later I got a call from Scot, the nicest member on the board. A likable younger guy with long hair, who was handpicked by the board as being the only one who might be able to talk some sense into me, Scot told me that they had rediscussed the proposal and that the attorneys had made an error. They were now looking at a number for me that would be one day worth about a million dollars.

The pendulum swung back, and all that leverage I'd had suddenly no longer mattered. Good old fear versus greed now had its full effect on me. If I didn't say yes, I'd have nothing—and that was my greatest fear. If I said yes, then I was accepting less than I was worth but far more money than I had ever had personally. That was a heavy dose of greed. I also knew this deal would build my reputation as a successful entrepreneur, and that in itself was worth millions.

I told them I'd think about it. And I did. In the end I knew that a million dollars would change my life, and having this deal on my bio would legitimize me as a start-up entrepreneur who could make his investors a great return. I started thinking that I could invest it wisely, maybe use the money to start another company and get my worth in the next venture. So the next time I walked into that boardroom, I sat down and signed my life away. I penned my signature to more than sixty documents, which head counsel witnessed. I took the fair deal, and left that room knowing that my life had completely changed. I'd made my investors a huge return, my customers had a better service provider, and my employees had better careers; and for me, my first deal was behind me.

After the sale, Nexweb, the company that had acquired us, made the Inc. 500 largely due to the revenue we handed them, and they offered me a job with some remedial title, as regional manager of sales or something. I took the job reluctantly, and I hated it. I came in late every day, and left early. I had little respect for my new bosses, and I just couldn't get behind the engineering culture that was so different from our entrepreneurial culture at SkyPipeline. They cared about their bits and bytes too much. The only bits I cared about were the butts in the seats of my employees' chairs.

I called Todd Goergen (one of the investors in SkyPipeline whom I liked a lot) to tell him that I was leaving. For some reason I just wanted to make sure we'd stay in touch. He was young, ambitious, and extremely smart, and I was straight with him. I said, "I'm calling you first because I want to do business with you in the future." I also told Todd how I really felt about some of the other board members and I used a lot of unflattering descriptions.

Todd laughed and said, "OK. Call me when you have something for me to look at."

After I left SkyPipeline, I spent the next couple of years living my dream life. I lost the sixty pounds I'd put on, and I got my health together. I moved to the beach and woke up to the sound of the ocean and watched sunrises that were the most beautiful I had ever seen. I dated girls who were previously out of my league. I bought a sports car, a new wardrobe, and jet-set the way this poor kid had always dreamed.

But my retirement wouldn't last long; I was burning cash fast. The aforementioned girls who were out of my league? Well, truth is they were. They were accustomed to guys who had far more wealth than I had, and I was fronting as if I were Diddy. The truth was I needed to get moving on my next project; otherwise I would soon find myself back at square one.

I wanted to do something different this time around. As I've mentioned, I tried the motivational speaking circuit but felt it was a scam. I started a business with a few armatures (see chapter 12, "Million-Dollar Mistakes") and it was a complete failure. I did some seminars, but it wasn't a way to make hundreds of millions, which I needed if I wanted to compete for the girls. I started doing media and landed a gig on *The Larry Elder Show* along with a few other notable appearances, and I wrote some articles. Then one day a guy I knew from my SkyPipeline days called me. Rich Pala was his name. He said he was working with two young extremely ambitious entrepreneurs who were looking for investors, and would I be interested?

I was interested. But the truth was, at that time I was about to run out of money, and I needed to get back to building a real business.

Rich set up a meeting with Nick Sarnicola and his company's CEO, Vito Terracciano. After they'd told me all about their company, ViSalus, I said, "Now that's something I can get passionate about." It was a company that made health products (I was into health and was taking lots of supplements back then) and it utilized independent sales representatives to sell its products. An entrepreneurial sales force that I could teach the subject I was most passionate about—entrepreneurship! It had potential to be more than my next business; it had the potential to be my lifelong passion.

It's funny, the first person I called when I left SkyPipeline was Todd, and coincidentally, the first person I called about ViSalus was Todd. The e-mail I sent is as follows:

From: Ryan J. Blair

Sent: Monday, March 07, 2005 5:30 PM

To: 'Todd Goergen'

Subject: RE: From Ryan J. Blair

Hey Todd,

Are you going to be in LA anytime soon? I want to pick your brain on direct sales models. I have completed an LBO on a wellness company called ViSalus that is using a direct sales model for distribution. The company has lots of promise. Please let me know your schedule. If you're not in LA anytime soon, I can come see you in NY. Hope all is well.

Ryan

After a few back-and-forth e-mails, Todd asked for the details behind the company, and here's the actual e-mail I sent him. You'll be able to tell as you read this that I was much more verbose back then, or as I would say to receiving an e-mail like this today, I was "green." I'm including this e-mail so that when you begin presenting your ideas to potential investors, you can use the details as a reference source.

From: Ryan J. Blair

Sent: Tuesday, March 22, 2005 7:31 AM

To: 'Todd Goergen'

Subject: Detail

Hey Todd,

Here's the detail behind the deal we put together. Let me know if this is something that you might be interested in. I'll get back to you with my NY schedule. Thanks for sending me your availability. Ryan

We very recently led a leveraged buyout of a Michigan based nutritional supplement company ViSalus Sciences upon which we acquired approximately $250,000 of hard assets and roughly $2,000,000 of soft assets. In the leveraged buyout plan, we only assumed approximately $100,000 worth of liabilities.

We put in $35,000 in cash to initiate the buyout. The transaction was completed on March 4, 2005, where the company agreed to pay $30,000 to the primary shareholder, Vitaliano Terracciano; $15,000 was paid on closing, with agreed terms to pay $5000 a month for the three following months. As part of the transaction we also agreed to pay a gross revenue pay out of up to 2.5%, but not to exceed 25k per month to the primary shareholder.

In the month of February (which was the acquisition month), ViSalus Sciences generated over $41,500 in total revenue,

yielding a $4,872 net profit. Despite March being a
transition month, the company projects and has month to
date results that indicate a 20-25% increase in gross
revenues. This will be a mild start, as the management team is
expecting to grow the company substantially over the next few
years and has laid the foundation for rapid scale through
its direct sales distribution model currently growing by over
20% per month.

In order to provide maximum value and commitment to the
company and its shareholders, the management team has
agreed to also merge their other personal ventures into the
holding company. These entities include an online goal setting
community known as PathConnect, and a live event production
company called Fusion. Fusion brings approximately $30,000
in assets and a recurring revenue stream of $100,000 annually.
Moving forward, all three entities, ViSalus Sciences,
PathConnect, and Fusion, will all fall under the legal
umbrella of the holding company, FVA Ventures, Inc.

PathConnect and Fusion have been in partnership under a Joint
Venture Agreement for approximately five months. This
partnership has been building a solid foundation for events,
seminars, sales aids, and PathConnect services. The activities of
PathConnect/Fusion are expected to produce an additional
$20,000 in revenue per month, yielding $10,000 in company
earnings during the month of March.

With all three entities merged into FVA Ventures, the company
expects that in the month of March alone, it will have an
operational profit of approximately $20,000.

Based on our very conservative forecasts, we anticipate the
company's net profit to clear over $100,000 a month by the end
of fiscal 05.

In the near future, the company will be raising $1,000,000 in equity financing to grow the scale of the company through enhanced sales and marketing resources.

As a result of the asset acquisition, we see minimum investment needed for manufacturing, product, fulfillment, software systems, or other operational infrastructure in order to greatly expand the company's sales and product distribution.

In order to cover the assumed liabilities and complete the merger of the companies we are offering a small investment opportunity of $150,000 to serve as a bridge equity financing to cover the approximate $100,000 in assumed liabilities, and $50,000 for working capital and operational costs to consolidate the operations of the combined companies.

I anticipate that we will cover the bridge with no more than 6 friends and family members. $25K each. The bridge loan financing will convert to preferred shares upon raising the aforementioned additional equity financing. During the bridge period (estimated to be 180 days) we will pay a deferred interest in the amount of 8%. Prior to completion of the company's Series A Preferred equity financing we will convert the bridge loans into the equity under the same terms of the financing. In addition to the 8% interest financing the company during its foundational period, we are willing to offer all bridge holders a 100% warrant to acquire an equal amount of shares at a discount of 20% from the share price established during the Series A financing for a period of 2 years (Series A Financing is estimated at $1 per share giving the combined companies a pre-money valuation of $1,000,000).

I am sending this e-mail to you because I feel that this is a great opportunity to become financially vested in three already profitable and healthy companies. With several people already interested I anticipate closing this transaction by the end of

business on March 30th. The value of the company is literally
growing daily. If you are interested, give me a call and we can
talk further.

Thanks,

Ryan J. Blair

After rereading this, "green" is an understatement.

Todd got back to me and we set up a meeting in New York on May 5,
2005, at the Racquet Club. That's when I had my second premonition.
Todd and I had a casual meeting over tea in New York. Two things were
notable about the meeting. First, Todd had a membership in the Racquet
Club and that's not an easy thing to get (for you *Wall Street* fans, this is
where Gordon Gekko schools Bud Fox about bringing him real insider
business information). Second, this was my first trip to New York and
this LA punk kid was in love with the pace of business and opportunity
that the city offered.

And just as Gekko had told Bud Fox in *Wall Street,* Todd told me to
come back with something much more exciting, like when the company
had $200,000 a month in sales. The only problem was, as you can see by
the e-mail, we were only doing about $40,000 a month and I had sent
him that e-mail in advance of flying all the way across the country. So
he had asked me to travel 2,795 miles to tell me something he could have
said via e-mail. My meeting with Todd lasted less than twenty minutes.

As opposed to taking this as an insult, or as a rejection, I saw it for
what it was. It was a test. Todd was testing my commitment to this venture. He was thinking that if I would get on a plane for a twenty-minute
meeting and then go home and build the venture up to $200,000 a
month, then he'd take a hard look. In my life I may never have passed
an academic test, but I never failed a test of will. And this was the ultimate test of will.

So in short, I had to improve sales fivefold so I could get Todd's private equity fund interested. So I went home to Los Angeles and called
my partners, the founders of ViSalus, Nick and Blake into a meeting. I

told them that the Goergens were going to invest and that Todd had arranged for me to meet his dad, a world-renowned venture capitalist, and
that if all went well, they would give us a few million dollars to build our
business. Note: That's called speaking into the future.

The only catch was that we had to get the company to $200,000 a
month, and fast.

I kept Todd informed of our progress every month, and on September
6, 2005, I sent him an e-mail stating that we were on target to cross over
the $200,000-per-month mark in that month.

His reply was:

> From: Todd Goergen
>
> Sent: Tuesday, September 06, 2005 5:31 PM
>
> To: Ryan J. Blair
>
> Subject: RE: From Ryan J. Blair
>
> Come meet my team in Greenwich on 9/16/05. Start around
> 11:00 am on Friday in Greenwich. My father and some folks
> from PartyLite will participate because we are in Greenwich.
>
> Plan on having dinner in NYC that night with me and one of my
> partners.
>
> TAG

I was elated. I had worked for six months to get this meeting, and
even longer, because technically I had worked with Todd since early
2002. Now the real work began.

First I had to create a presentation that would motivate the Goergen
team to invest. I had to package my company, convey its strategy, and
persuade some of the smartest people in the world to get behind me and
my team. And these smart people knew more about my business than I
did. I worked every minute, from the moment I got notice of the meeting

to the minute I showed up for the presentation to the Goergen family at Blyth World Headquarters.

I'll never forget walking into Blyth HQ. I remember walking past a collage of framed stock certificates on the wall, which for some reason I was drawn to. As I walked over to it, I was greeted by Bob Goergen himself. I was so nervous. This was one of the Forbes 400 richest Americans, a real icon, and he was walking right toward me wearing his Armani suit and impeccable shoes. I immediately noticed his gold Rolex. He said to me, "You know what that is, right?"

"No sir," I replied.

"Those are failed investments. Guys like you, whom we bought into but failed to perform."

I reexamined the stocks and the letters hanging on the wall. Letters from CEOs saying things like, "Dear Mr. Goergen, the following 100 shares should be worth tens of millions!"

I remember thinking, *There is no way—I won't be immortalized on that wall!* I had no idea that the very stock I would sell him that day eventually would become about as worthless as wallpaper.

The meeting started and I gave my presentation at the end. Bob Goergen asked me, "How much money do you need, Ryan?" I said, "I need a minimum of $1.5 million."

He shrugged off the number and said, "We're in, under these conditions: get through due diligence, hire a solid finance guy, and our name can't be involved at this stage." I would later learn that those conditions would require another four months of twenty-four-hour days, but for a shot at greatness, it would all be worth it. And as the song "Lose Yourself" by Eminem goes, "If you had one shot. . . ."

After the meeting I got into the town car they'd arranged for me and we drove through Greenwich, Connecticut. Apart from what I'd read about Greenwich, I'd never been to a place like that. Here I was driving past one billionaire's home after the next, after having met with one of the most influential men in the world. I was in the midst of daydreaming when I got that same rush I had gotten when I knew I'd sell SkyPipeline.

This time I knew that one day Bob Goergen was going to buy ViSalus. In that car ride I visualized it, and I knew that I was on the path to my destiny.

That following Monday I began to work on the conditions they had imposed. That Saturday I sent Nick and Blake the following e-mail:

From: Ryan J. Blair

Sent: Saturday, September 24, 2005 7:40 AM

To: nsarnicola; 'Blake Mallen'

Subject: Massive attack

Guys, let's kill this shit . . . We need the money in the bank! We're at 91K! Let's hit all of our goals and impress the Goergens and make them want to do a deal so bad that we sell less of the company for more money.

If we beat our numbers . . . I might be able to make part of the deal that we each get to take 100K off the table from the transaction. The more money we make this month the more room I have to work with.

Let's create a cause this weekend and get our team so behind it . . . that they hit their numbers or die trying!

Kill ▮▮▮▮!!

Kill ▮▮▮▮!!!

Kill em all!

CHEERS.

Ryan J. Blair

Nobody believes you when you speak into the future. Very few people are able to see a clear path like that and follow it. I used to tell Nick and Blake all the time that one day Blyth would buy ViSalus. I saw that straight shot and I took it. I seized the day and they did their part to make sure that day would come.

Since the Goergens had invested in us, Blyth had found a way to eavesdrop on ViSalus. They'd send someone to drop in at a board meeting, audit our events, review our financials, and make sure they tracked us.

One day I straight out asked Todd, "What are the chances that Blyth will buy us?"

Todd said, "Little."

I didn't buy the odds. My vision was clear.

In February 2008, Blyth sent one of their executives to audit a ViSalus conference. I sat down with him when it was over and I told him that I had other buyers at the table. In fact, I was in negotiations with several funds that wanted a piece of our deal. I had term sheets in hand, and I said that if Blyth wanted the opportunity to buy us, they should jump on it now. He went back and told the Goergens that the little company they'd invested in had grown up.

On April 17, 2008, I was summoned for another presentation to Bob Goergen and the Blyth team. I started the meeting with this opening remark: "Three years ago to the day I came here to ask you for millions of dollars to help build ViSalus into the company it was capable of being. Nothing has changed except the number of zeros I'm looking for."

Bob Goergen literally laughed out loud. And his ensemble of suits followed suit.

I knew they would buy it, but I had no idea about the kind of test I would go through to close the deal. They put me through the craziest due diligence, through hell and back, and then when I thought I couldn't take any more, they required that I divest PathConnect, which involved letting go of twenty employees and possibly burning the $2.5 million several investors and I had put into the company along the way. They also required that I test and retest and relabel and remanufacture every product we made. I had to hire tax advisers, corporate attorneys, personal attorneys, FDA attorneys, and FTC attorneys; and all those attorneys had to deal with their counterparts on the other side of the deal. We spent more than a million on attorneys and fees. (See chapter 18 under "Lawyer Up.")

At one point, every step I made was through fear, because I knew if they pulled the plug on the acquisition, I wouldn't have enough money to stay in business. I was doing the deal because I needed working capital in the first place and now this deal was not only costing us more than $1 million in fees, it was also costing our management's focus on building the business, in a time when the economy was changing rapidly. Remember, this was just days before the 2008 recession. This is when having a nothing-to-lose mind-set comes into play. I just focused and kept charging ahead, and played my highest-stakes game of poker to date. I went all in.

Term after term, we negotiated. One time we were discussing the revision of the contract and I noticed some of the same terms that had been the result of that zero calculation from the sale of SkyPipeline. It took me back to the anger I'd felt in that boardroom with those investors, and I leaned on that feeling. We called the Blyth negotiators and said, "The terms are unacceptable. Either accept our terms and send back the documents or the whole deal is off."

A rather loud bluff, but the only move we could make in this situation. I wasn't going to swallow the same poison pill that had nearly killed me in my last deal. After all, I wasn't building my résumé here, I was building my life's mission.

We told their attorneys, "Go back and tell your boss that this whole thing fell apart because you guys are being greedy." I remember that I was so adamant, one of the Blyth attorneys said on the phone, "Calm down! Nobody is trying to insult you."

They suggested a day to review the matter, then they came back and accepted our terms. And the rest was history. The premonition I had had that day in the town car while leaving Blyth's HQ was now a reality.

I'm sharing these stories with you not to impress you but to show you that life is a summary of actions taken. If I could have enough faith to believe in my goals and become the person I once dreamed of being, and build a company that someone would one day buy for millions of dollars, so can you.

But first you have to learn how to honor your deals.

# 6

## HONOR YOUR DEALS

———————

One time I made the mistake of living beyond my means. I was driving a hundred-thousand-dollar sports car and living in a beach home overlooking the ocean, but I had a negative bank balance and my credit cards were completely maxed out. I remember thinking that I couldn't even take a girl out on a date and fill up my gas tank. I'd completely squandered my money on a failed investment (which I'll talk about later in chapter 12, "Million-Dollar Mistakes"). I had bet all my liquid cash on that venture, and then, tail between my legs, I had to ask my stepfather for a loan.

This was against Bob's principles. If you knew Bob, you knew that he always wanted the best price on everything. He said I'd been living irrationally.

After having learned how the business world was structured, I couldn't fathom working for a manager who worked for another entrepreneur. Besides, I had no career training, no college degree. Regardless, I told Bob that if he wouldn't lend me the money, I would have to shutter my entrepreneurial dreams and get an actual job.

Reluctantly, almost angrily, he grabbed his checkbook and said, "Ryan, you're unemployable. Trust me. You used to work for me."

He was frustrated that he'd broken his own personal rule and lent money to a family member. He knew what it must have taken out of me to ask for help, and maybe I'd learn the lesson.

Bob lent me $20,000, and his terms were very gracious: 8 percent interest. I had to take on a 1099 for the loan amount, and I would receive a daily call as a reminder that I was late. When I finally paid him back (with principal and interest), it was a proud moment because never again would I have shame on my face at a family gathering, or have to worry that the next incoming call was from my bill collector stepfather, Bob.

To Bob, a deal was a deal, and he taught me to honor my deals. True to his word, a month after I'd paid him back he called to tell me I'd miscalculated the interest. I owed him $67. He was a true businessman and a man of his word, and I will miss him very much.

We recently lost Bob to lung cancer. At the long bedside vigils while Bob was dying, I got my last chance to make a deal with my stepfather.

He'd been checked into the hospital with pneumonia on a weekend. Two days later he was diagnosed with lung cancer that had metastasized to his brain, and he would die within that week. After days of watching my stepfather's numerous friends make emotional visits to his hospital room, and watching the unstoppable decay of his mental acuity, the family made a decision. I pulled every string to get the right equipment and the staff, and we took him home to die. There in his own home I sat with him, hand in hand, for ten- and twelve-hour stretches. I had dropped everything to spend every last minute with the man who had rescued my mother and given me all I had.

Late into the night, knowing that a person's hearing was the last of the senses to go, I leaned in and whispered into my stepfather's ear. I told him, "I always sought your approval. Everything I ever did was to impress you." I said, "You were my true father. I'm going to make you proud and take care of my mother when you're gone. I will honor my commitments."

He grabbed my arm tight, pulled me close, and said, "I'm proud of you."

It hit me that I would never try to impress this man again. What all sons dream of doing is making their dads proud. I'd gotten final praise from a man who had never congratulated me for my achievements, only for my potential. And it wasn't because of my art collection, or my cars, or my millions, or all the other things I'd bragged about to him over the years. It was because I'd just stepped up for my family. He'd taken care of my mom so that I could concentrate on becoming the man I am today, and now he could pass in peace, knowing that I would take responsibility for her.

And she will be cared for, because I've learned how to honor my deals. Often, the hard way.

Having been raised spiritually, I was always taught to pray and hope for the best; that when you are down on your luck, get down on your knees and pray. As a kid I often prayed for my mom and dad to sober up. I'd pray that we wouldn't lose our house. I'd pray for my father's rage to stop. My prayers were never answered in the way I wanted, but still I held on to the belief that the only person you can turn to when you're down is God.

By the time I was seventeen I'd been arrested nearly ten times; I'd been asked to shoot a man to prove myself to the gang I was accepted in; I'd broken into and robbed every business within a mile radius from my house; I'd been dragged home in the middle of the night by police officers; I'd sold firearms with disastrous results; I'd gotten convicted for strong-arm robbery. Finally, after many of these episodes, I found myself sitting in a jail cell in Juvenile Hall, faced with four years. Every day I watched people leave the jail and wished I were among them. I got more and more depressed. I made use of my time by writing in my journal and writing letters to my family, and true to my upbringing, I started making deals. First I made deals with God, then I made deals with myself, and finally I started making deals with my mother and everybody else.

Shortly after I appeared in court that August 1993, I wrote a letter thanking my mother for being there for me. It said, "Mom . . . I am making an oath that I will do better. I am going to go to school, get a job and make you proud. I am sorry for what I did, I truly am."

My mother wrote me back, saying, "Dear Ryan, just a note. It was good to be with you on Wednesday. I love you and care about you very much. I miss the Ryan that was good and caring and kind to people. I hope you have learned a lesson. That you realize that you were wrong in what you were doing and did. We'll see you soon on Sunday, Grandma is coming with me. Take care of yourself and do the right thing. Love, Mom."

When you're facing four years, surrounded by people who have nothing to lose because they're going to prison for the rest of their lives—some of them for taking lives—there is nothing left to do but make deals. Eventually one of those deals paid off.

I had the idea to write a letter to Judge Perrin, the head of juvenile justice, in an effort to convince him of my change of heart. Judge Perrin had a reputation for taking no prisoners (or taking prisoners, as it were), but it was worth a try because I had nothing to lose. My penmanship was so bad back then because of my learning disabilities and the healthy dose of Prozac the juvenile hall counselors put me on, I had to recruit one of my cellmates to write it for me. In perfect old English cursive the letter read: "Dear Honorable Judge Perrin, I'm writing you this letter because I want you to know that I am truly sorry for what I have done. It was wrong and I admit it. I'm aware of the consequences I must face. Not only did I hurt Mr. Andrews, but for that matter, I've hurt my family, too.

"I've been in here twenty-six days. I want you to know I learned a lesson when I first came in front of the court on July 30th. The D.D.A. Karen Block referred to me as a burden to society. I want you to know I'm no longer a burden, but an asset to society. I plan to continue my education, start family counseling and become a responsible law-abiding citizen. I realize I have to control my anger or else I'll be unsuccessful in life.

"Your Honor, I'm asking you for a chance. I give you my word I'll never see you under these circumstances again. Thank you for giving me the opportunity to show my true feelings. I'm deeply sorry for what I've done. Thank you for your time. Sincerely, Ryan Jerry Blair."

Judge Perrin did take the time to read my letter and gave me leniency. I got the chance to honor the deal I'd made. But this isn't a fairy tale where an angel came down and handed me a pot of gold. I got out of jail and, of course, immediately called my homeys. But this time, at least, I knew I was dishonoring the deals I'd made. I knew I wasn't doing the right thing.

As we grow and develop into the citizens we desire to be, we don't always honor every deal we make right away. We don't have control over all the circumstances. We don't have control over the expectations other people have. Someone will always feel you did him wrong. But you do your best to honor your deals, regardless.

Circumstances change. For example, people will be relying on you for employment and maybe suddenly your new board of directors doesn't give a shit about the deal you made. Or maybe the market changes. Maybe you took out a loan, but your company wasn't in a position to pay it back in the time you thought it could. Maybe you just failed to perform. That happens. We all have the capacity to take on something, thinking it's going to end up a certain way, and then it doesn't. Next thing you know, you haven't honored a deal. The most important thing is to ask yourself how to make it right, then how to make sure you don't do it again.

You have to bank the lesson and figure out how to restructure the situation so it never recurs. For instance, I told one of the first employees I hired at SkyPipeline that "if all goes well, you'll be rich from the equity you own in the company."

What he heard was "Ryan said I'm going to be rich no matter what."

It was a pretty broad statement, and an overly optimistic one. The problem is that as you start to add more and more individuals to the equation, everyone has to perform equally to get their equal, or more than equal, share. Suddenly this employee's performance didn't warrant additional equity incentives because there were others who were contributing more to the team.

The lesson here was not to create false expectations or make vague promises with regard to cash, salary, or equity. Of course this is really hard to do when you want everyone, including yourself, to believe that you're all going to be millionaires.

Or maybe you've got a multimillion-dollar idea, but you didn't structure it correctly, as I've mentioned, and you have to break a deal.

One time a businessman approached me for some advice. This guy had a great idea based solely on his ability to life coach tens of thousands of people. He'd raised all kinds of money, and lots of people had invested in his grand vision. He'd raised upward of $600,000.

He raised it all on a grandiose, overly optimistic business plan that didn't mature, and now he had hundreds of people who hated him. Some of whom had given him their life savings. He wasn't a scam artist; he just didn't know what he was doing. This was a case of pure negligence.

Unfortunately, I didn't have a great solution for him, other than to say business is business, and that's why there's bankruptcy law. I felt bad, though. I told him to write a letter to each of his investors, explaining to them what had happened, that the business hadn't matured or materialized in the way he had thought it would, and that he was going to take responsibility by carrying their investment with interest into his next venture. He'd have to figure out a way, no matter what, to make it right.

I call that making a new deal. If you can't honor the first deal, make a new one and do whatever it takes to honor it.

There will be times, of course, when you honor a deal and get screwed. For example, one time there was a sales rep from my company who had gotten himself into a jam with the company he'd left. He asked me if I would help him pay his attorney's fees.

I didn't take the time to explain to him that there would be a process for taking this matter to the board. I thought that when the time came to take it to the board members, it would be easy. I said yes, reluctantly, knowing that if I couldn't get my board and partners to participate, I'd either have to break my deal or get stuck holding the bag.

It did fall onto me, and I did honor it. I gave him $50,000 of my own money because I had made a commitment to honor the deal I'd made with him. It was a black-and-white case. I said I'd figure out how to help him when he came to me, and I had to honor the commitment. My board would have been very angry with this deal based on the result, and it wasn't worth embarrassing myself over $50,000.

I wrote that check and he cashed it. He immediately started using my own money to recruit against me when he joined another company. We later sued the guy and he owes me ten times the amount I'd loaned him, thanks to the terms we'd set if he breached the agreement. I don't antici-pate ever profiting or receiving my money back from that deal, although there's a lawsuit against him and a team of attorneys waiting to suck the money out of any bank account he opens for the rest of his life.

If I could go back and do it over again, I wouldn't have made the deal in the first place. And although I'm not litigious, I will sue someone out of principle, and I'll make it hurt, because even worse than having a reputation as someone who doesn't honor his deals is having a reputa-tion as someone who can be taken in business. If you can be taken, you will be. And no one steals my milk.

The lesson in this chapter is obvious—if you want to be successful, you have to honor your deals. I am still earning dividends from deals I made a decade ago. But be careful what you take on, and try to learn from my shortsightedness. If you can't honor a deal, make a new one and try to honor it. And when you're dealing with your investors' money, you have to act as if God himself wrote you the check.

# 7

## SMARTEN UP

---

**A**cross the audience of thirty, a kid who'd raised his hand caught my attention. I pointed to him. He said, "I'm in jail. How am I supposed to become a millionaire like you?"

Good question.

I was standing in front of a room full of young men at the Judge Perrin Juvenile Detention Center, where I'd been invited to speak about the role entrepreneurship played in turning my life around. I had no idea what I was going to say to them when I got there, or where I'd start. Truthfully, I wasn't prepared for how overwhelmed I would be by my surroundings.

The original structure had been torn down years earlier and replaced by the building I was standing in, but even so, things were still the same. The cells were the same. I remembered sitting in them, sometimes twenty-three hours at a time in solitary confinement for fighting, counting the dots in the ceiling panels. I read my first book in those cells, and reread it until I could practically recite it from memory. The jumpsuits were the same, the smell was the same, and the guards were the same (much to my surprise, one of them recognized me). It had been eighteen years.

"The first thing you guys have to do is smarten up," I said, addressing his question. We handed out a first draft of *Nothing to Lose* to every inmate that day. "Take this book and read it. Some of the concepts will be over your head, but read it over and over. Write up a list of questions as you're reading it.

"Learning how to become an entrepreneur, like learning anything, is going to be complex and overwhelming at first. What if someone told you that if you took an ax and dug a hole in the ground every day for eighteen years, there would be millions of dollars waiting for you at the end. Would you do it? Wouldn't anyone do it?

"When my mother started dating my stepfather Bob, he gave me two rules: I had to go back to school and get my high school diploma, and I had to get a job. He was telling me I had to smarten up."

I've never passed a math aptitude test in my life. I read my first book when I was already a teenager in juvie. I dropped out of high school with hardly enough credits to be considered a freshman. To this day, I have a hard time with spelling, because of my dyslexia I couldn't visualize words properly in my head.

The idea of going back to school was terrifying. But I couldn't jeopardize my chance for a better life, so I did it.

Back in high school I realized something important: I wasn't a visual learner. I can't see something and then remember it, but I can hear something and recite it word for word. Even when I read, I don't picture what I'm reading in my mind, but there is a voice inside my head narrating each sentence on the page. I got a tape recorder and started recording my classes, and the recordings allowed me to come back to the information every time my attention span had gotten off track. I finally started making progress.

My stepfather decided to give me his own type of education. He gave me an audiotape series called *Lead the Field* by Earl Nightingale. His challenge to me was this: if I listened to the tapes and could pass his quiz at the end of it, he would take me clothes shopping so I could get a good job.

The only way I can describe Earl Nightingale's voice is to say that he sounds like an old radio announcer. For a kid who listened to nothing but rap like Snoop Dogg, Eazy-E, and Dr. Dre, it was a pretty big step to sit down and let some old white guy tell me that "you can do it" and that "attitude is everything."

But it was important enough for me to impress my stepfather, and besides, I had nothing to lose. So I put aside my judgments and listened for the key lessons. I even went to sleep listening to the tapes every night, and had dreams in the voice of Earl Nightingale.

When it came time for my stepfather's test, I knew the material by heart.

The one-size-fits-all learning environment in school had turned out a miserable failure of a student until I figured out my learning style. Since then, I can now turn on my focus anytime I need to retain information, whether I'm sitting in a movie theater, listening to a song, or participating in a meeting with my management team.

We love to dream of the day when we've finally "made it"—when there is nothing left to do, nothing left to worry about, nothing left to learn. Unfortunately, for an entrepreneur, that day will never come. You, the reader, also have to figure out your individual learning strategy, because if you want to be successful, you're going to have to become a lifelong student. And at the pace of technological advancements, you'll need to learn quickly to apply those lessons to keep up in business.

Throughout my early twenties, I continued feeding myself information according to the style of learning I had discovered. One day I stumbled across a tape of one of Tony Robbins's speeches. I was mesmerized. He was so dynamic and engaging that I hung on his every word, wanting not only to understand everything he was saying, but also to learn how he was doing it—what made him so convincing, so trustworthy, and so likable.

I read and studied everything about him I could find, I interviewed his ex-employees, and I watched his tapes; and the more I learned, the more I realized that he was an act. Sure, he believed what he was selling, and I did find his concepts credible, but come on, could a guy really be that perfect? After getting my hands on some of his "behind the scenes" tapes, I realized that the guy on the television cursed like a sailor and was actually a hustler, just like me. I didn't like his act, but when I peeled back the layers, his core was real. I respected who he was when the cameras weren't on (or at least when he didn't know they were on).

I knew that someday, that was what I wanted to do. I wanted to empower people. I wanted to tell my story and help others overcome their stories. Tony Robbins represented everything that I wanted to do, and he did it better than anyone else. So I studied him and smartened up.

There is a reason why we admire certain people. They espouse something that strikes a chord within us. Be it their innate talent, drive, wisdom, or attitude, there is a reason we find certain individuals fascinating, and if we can harness that same spark that made them great, perhaps we can achieve greatness as well. In some cases, like this one, I even admire my competition.

We all have heroes.

I read every blog, trade magazine, and book, and listen to anyone telling the story of an individual who is successful in any category I have interest in. In fact today my good friend was telling me about an article in *Rolling Stone* about how Marshall Mathers (Eminem) got over the death of his best friend. I went out and found the back issue of *Rolling Stone* because at the time I was going through the death of my stepfather, and I figured I could learn something from how he rebounded from his lows. Besides, I've always identified with Marshall, his path to success, and the difficulty he had in overcoming that.

After reading the article, I penned him a note with an advance copy of this book. This is an example of how I'm reaching out to my heroes, creating common interest and connection.

I use this type of approach, whether it's a book I've written or a book I've read, with anyone I want to do business with and learn from— whether it's a fortune 500 CEO or Emmy award–winning musician.

## WHO'S YOUR *MENTOREN*?

When I toured Norway in 2008, the Norwegian *Financial Times* (*Finansavisen*, Oslo) featured me in an article. Across the two-page spread of my ugly mug was the word *mentoren*. I thought it was funny because it sounded so superhero-like, and in real life a mentor isn't necessarily a superhero. Aim high, but don't wait for a super businessman to save your day. Find a mentor, any mentor, to help show you the ropes and refine your ideas. Find anyone better than you are at what you want to do, and start there.

I've been extremely fortunate because my first mentor was my stepfather, Robert Hunt. I got to learn how to create definitions for success, how to be a good father and husband, how to run a business, and how to live a life fulfilled—all by watching up close and in person a man who embodied all of these attributes and more.

My nature is introverted, and even though I'm comfortable speaking in front of the largest audiences, I won't always say hi to everyone at a party. It's not that I don't care, I just feel awkward. And if I do say hi to everyone, it's only because I know that everyone will think I'm rude if I don't. Bob was the best extrovert I've ever met, the opposite of me. He'd say hello to everyone at the party, and good bye to everyone before he left. He'd throw his arms out and hug people, and they loved it.

That was something Bob did naturally, and his warmth yielded him very successful relationships both in business and his personal life. Again and again I watched the way people responded to his hugs and handshakes. How he would do favors for people and how glad they were to do things for him in return. It made his life easier. Bob was my model for creating successful relationships with people, and I learned how to adapt my behavior in order to get the same results.

With or without realizing it, every successful person has created behaviors—systems for greeting people, networking, and making telephone calls to aid them in their pursuits. By observing the traits of successful people, you can create your own system for success.

As I said, I got lucky when I found my first mentor. But if you haven't been so fortunate to have one in your immediate network, how do you find the right person to teach you?

You have to be willing to at least write a letter, make a phone call, or reach out in some way to ask for a meeting. If you don't at least try, you'll never even have the chance.

I meet people through networking. I go to charity events or attend conferences in my industry. And when someone seems as if she could mentor me on a subject I could use some help on, I go to work thinking of how I could add value to her life in return for her help. The key is in how you approach people, and how well you've prepared.

Here's an example from personal experience. Because I speak at many of these events, I have had individuals approach me afterward and say things like, "Ryan, here's my card with my contact information. What you said was extremely relevant to my business. My goal is to learn everything I possibly can about this industry because I want to build a very successful company within it. Do you mind if I take two or three minutes of your time to learn a few things from you?"

My answer is always that I'd be happy to give that person a few minutes of my time because it is clear to me that he will have targeted specific questions. If I feel he's going to be vague, I won't reply.

Think about what would happen if Michael Jordan were to sit down for an interview with a sports journalist who said, "Oh my gosh, you're just the best! Can you teach me how to be a successful basketball player?" He'd probably just smile and give some generic answer like, "Thanks. The secret to success is to work hard and never give up on your dreams." But if that same journalist were to say, "I've studied your game, and I notice that in certain circumstances, you tend to prefer X technique, which goes against conventional wisdom. Clearly it worked for you, though—would you mind explaining why you chose to play that way?" Suddenly the reporter has Jordan's attention because he is demonstrating his own level of proficiency in the game as well as exhibiting specific knowledge of the person from whom he is seeking guidance.

Specific questions are much more likely to lead to specific answers, but to ask those kinds of questions, you have to be fully knowledgeable about the subject area and the person you're addressing. You should research the person thoroughly—read every newspaper or magazine article printed about her, try to track down each TV or radio interview she's done, and learn whatever you can about her company. Only by doing your homework will you be in a position to ask the right kinds of questions that will set you apart from the other people seeking mentorship. If you show you've done your homework, the person will be impressed and engage with you. Showing her that you put in the time is a compliment to her.

And this is what I call being a student of your industry.

Here's a proverb that might help: Never ask a question you can find the answer to otherwise. Find out company statistics and the basics of the person's life through the various Internet resources available. Don't waste your time or hers with questions that can be learned through research.

I recently received a great interview tip from Coach Dale Brown. When he was offered his first head coach position in 1972, he made a list of people he wanted to interview who had the standards of speaking, public relations, and coaching that he hoped to incorporate into his own program. At the top of his list was legendary UCLA basketball coach John Wooden.

But when Dale sat down to come up with a list of questions to ask this icon of his sport, he froze up and was completely at a loss as to where he should even start. Finally, he pulled out a notebook and wrote down the alphabet, using each letter to prompt ideas for his questions. When he went out to visit Coach Wooden, he ended up staying for five days and filling several notebooks full of advice and wisdom on a wide variety of issues, thanks to his alphabet notes. I used this technique to interview Coach Brown himself, and I can tell you it worked. Today, you can find that interview on www.youtube.com/nothingtolosevideo.

Most of us will not be privileged enough to get five whole days with our mentors, but you don't need five days if you prepare correctly.

Another great way to make connections is through charity work. Any smart, ethical business owner is going to be involved with something that gives back, whether it is at the community level, in the fight against a specific disease, or in a broad campaign to address another social issue. If you are willing to take the time to roll up your sleeves—first, to find out what groups your targeted mentor works with, and second, to start giving your money, time, or resources to that same group—you can find inroads to business mentors very quickly, and all while pursuing a worthy cause.

My work with nonprofits has yielded me some great connections. One charity I support is Urban Born, a Los Angeles–based organization that helps kids get off the streets and learn the art of filmmaking. I was introduced to it by hip-hop mogul Percy Miller, who I met through this book. When we first sat down to talk, he told me about his philanthropic work with Urban Born and said, "We're both successful, we're both wealthy—I'll endorse your book, but show me that you're not just about money and give back."

Without giving it another thought, I grabbed my checkbook and stroked him $100,000. I said, "Here's the first half of my gift to Urban Born. The second half will come once you set up a program to teach these kids entrepreneurship." He was absolutely shocked: He knows a lot of successful people, and when he's asked them to donate to his charity, which he's very passionate about, they've given him nothing but excuses. I did it because I was also passionate about what the charity supported— kids growing up under the same circumstances I did. And I did it because I wanted to gain his trust and do business with him. We have worked together ever since.

Not all of you are going to be able to give $200,000 to a hip-hop mogul right now, but you can donate your time and energy to charities that inspire you. Mentors like Percy and me would rather hear you talk about the causes you're passionate about and how you're going to give back than talk about yourself.

At the end of your life you're going to give it all away, anyway. It's just a matter of to whom and with what instructions you give it. So, give your time and money away to causes while you can—you'll make a lot of friends along the way and a make a difference in the world.

Isn't that what entrepreneurship is all about? Your network is money. Be smart about it.

But here's the thing: not everyone is going to say yes. Not every potential mentor is going to respond positively to your introduction or answer your letter. I was recently rejected when I didn't follow my own advice and reached out to someone without reciprocal value to offer. (One day Warren Buffett will take my call.) And when that is the case, move on to the next 999 people who are relevant to your company. Once you look into it, you'll find that there really is a long list of people from whom you could draw some form of mentorship. Search until you find the right match of relevant experience and knowledge, and the right chemistry between you and that person. You might very well hit it off with the person and end up saying, "We know some of the same people" or "We went to the same college." You know you've hit the jackpot when the mentor you seek says, "You remind me of myself when I was at that stage in my career." I'll never forget when Russ Bik, a founder of Sun Microsystems, said that to me. When you make those kinds of connections, that's when you have an open invitation to take the next step of asking for business mentorship.

Fred Warren was just such a mentor for me. When he first took an interest in SkyPipeline, he saw a company with a lot of potential being run by a kid who had very little experience. He recognized that with a little training—sometimes in the form of encouragement and sometimes in the form of tough love—I had the potential to be a very successful entrepreneur.

Fred did a lot for me. He introduced me to leaders of several successful companies so I could see how they managed their businesses, how they leveraged deals, and how they interacted with colleagues and customers. Occasionally he would call my attention to a situation he felt needed to be addressed, but that I might not have had enough experience to recognize or know how to handle appropriately.

The lessons were tough ones to learn sometimes. But because of the wisdom he was able to offer from decades of experience, I was able to avoid a lot of rookie mistakes that might have cost me far more time and money than I could afford. I did make a few million-dollar mistakes under his mentorship; however, I made several more good million-dollar decisions. Sometimes I was thickheaded, sometimes I would argue with him, and sometimes I would fight with him. But looking back, I realize that he was usually right; now I give Fred a lot of credit for teaching me how to be a CEO. My relationship with him lasted just about three years. I got just enough of Fred to know what I didn't know, and he got just enough of me to make several million dollars.

As Fred would say to this day, "I broke my pick on you, Ryan."

I can name at least twenty people who have given me specific life-changing wisdom and advice that I have used to become a better person. Some of my mentors spent more time with me than others. Some I learned from only once, but they have forever contributed to my life: my very first technology mentor, my first venture capitalist mentors. Others were longer term: my mother and my stepfather, of course, and even my deadbeat dad. The lessons these people have taught me about what to do, how to think, and what to value—as well as mistakes to avoid—have shaped the person I am. There have been countless others who have changed my life and are still changing it today.

Recently a man who saw me speak at the University of Oregon drove twenty hours one way to have a thirty-minute meeting with me, and had even offered to intern for ninety days with me if I would just mentor him. He then drove back twenty more hours. Now, that took tenacity and total commitment, and I was impressed. I gave him ninety days of mentorship and continue to give him an opinion or two when asked. In short, if you really want it, then give it everything you have and don't hold back.

And finally, use your powers of observation. Sometimes the things we learn from our heroes aren't the lessons we expected. For instance, I used to be really impressed by the typical status symbols in our culture. I was absolutely in awe if someone had a Ferrari parked out front, or was sporting a Rolex. That meant they had made it—that meant they were truly successful, right?

Several years ago, I held an event at my place and one of the attendees happened to be Paul Allen, the cofounder of Microsoft and certainly the richest, most successful person who had ever set foot in my home. But the most impressive thing about Paul Allen wasn't the way he was dressed or the car he drove. It was his humility.

The artist whose paintings I have hanging on my living room walls approached Paul while he was curiously examining one of the pieces. I happened to be standing with Paul as they struck up a casual conversation about art and work, and I overheard my artist friend ask Paul what he did for a living. He smiled cheerfully and replied, "I'm in the computer industry"—certainly a very humble answer for a man who has every right in the world to brag about himself, and an example to follow.

You can tell a lot about a person by his or her prized possession. Besides the artwork I own, the items I collect are not what would fetch a fortune at Sotheby's. Rather than things intended to impress someone else, my collection reminds me of the people who taught me to be a better businessman, employer, philanthropist, and person.

I have first-edition signed copies of the two books that meant the most to me when I was first starting out: *Think and Grow Rich* by Napoleon Hill, and *How to Win Friends and Influence People* by Dale Carnegie. I collect all kinds of artifacts of greatness. I have letters from JFK, jerseys signed by championship teams, and a framed copy of John Wooden's pyramid of success. I have photos with Coach Dale Brown, who has been like a father to me. I have a picture of my mom and me when I was six years old—it was the day she told me that I could be anything I wanted to be. These are the things I surround myself with. Their purpose is to remind me to ask myself daily whether or not I am living up to the lessons learned from each person along the way.

And sometimes when I fall off track I only need to look at the books on my shelf, or call the mentors in my Rolodex to smarten up.

# 8

## FIRST THINGS FIRST

---

**B**ack when I had just started my career, disaster struck. In a panic I rushed into my boss's office to explain. "The servers didn't come back up," I said. There'd been a power outage at the data center where I was in charge, and even though we'd got the power back on, some of the servers still weren't responding.

My boss was tough, and I knew those servers generated thousands of dollars an hour in revenue; I thought for sure I was going to lose my job. He just looked at me and said, "That's the problem, but what's the solution?" He then told me that if all I ever did was bring him problems, and not solutions, I *would* lose my job.

I banked that lesson and I still apply it, to this day. As entrepreneurs or company executives, we need to be solution oriented. Businesses exist in the first place as solutions to problems.

The bigger your company gets, the more you are going to be faced with slow sales, fast sales, scaling issues, employee issues, competition issues, crises, chaos, and more problems than you ever could have dreamed. It's going to be overwhelming.

I remember when things would go bad and I would shut my office

door and not come out. And then I would look at the Mark Twain quote
that hung over my desk, one of my personal Golden Rules that you'll
remember from chapter 4: "The secret of getting ahead is getting
started. . . ."

So I'd start by writing down the problem and every remedy I could
think of to solve it. Then I would analyze each solution and eliminate
those that didn't solve the problem fast enough, or efficiently enough (for
example, the solution might cost too much money), until I had a plan of
action. Today over my desk there is a simple maxim I came up with to
calm myself when I'm overwhelmed: "The path is all math," meaning
there's an equation that will lead to your answers. You just have to find
it. The equation will lead to the shortest, most efficient solution and will
then prioritize the tasks necessary to get the problem solved.

As I'm writing this, ViSalus is growing very fast, and we're having
scaling issues. We went from adding twelve thousand customers a year
to nearly twice that number a week. One of my mentors used to call
problems like this happy trouble, but there's nothing particularly happy
about building a business model that works so well that your infrastructure can't support it.

For example, in our call center, we're experiencing significant hold
times because of the vast number of calls we receive daily from distributors and customers. It's worrisome because the hold times can be half
an hour long, and people are starting to complain. An entrepreneur who
won't last long is one who will respond to this type of crisis with emotion, perhaps by throwing bodies at the problem, overhiring and killing
profits.

The path is math. Hire someone to look at the data and study the
analytics. When is the highest call volume occurring, and where is it
coming from? Is there a way to survey the customers to find out why the
majority are calling? Can their questions be answered via e-mail, online
chat, or in some other way?

I used this example not to try to teach you how to scale a call center,
but to show you that the problem can be solved with math, not emotion.
That's it.

Also "inspect what you expect" and follow up on action items; make sure that everyone knows what's on your mind. Even if I have to sound like a broken record, my employees will hear the company's number one priority until the problem is solved.

The technique I use to manage my day today is similar: I obsess over the most critical goal or obstacle until I can't think about anything else. That's why I titled this chapter "First Things First." Write down a list of everything you believe is critical to the success of your business and then focus on the one item that will save you the most money or generate the most money. Work on the task until it's completed or until some outside dependency requires you to wait (such as getting a quote from a vendor or the arrival of a shipment), then work on something else and come back to the first when the outside dependency is fulfilled.

It sounds simple, but it isn't—especially if you're like me and you're creative. You want to do all kinds of other cool stuff instead. Don't be afraid to kill a project halfway through if you realize that it's not the company's highest priority.

At ViSalus, we were in the middle of developing a product called Neuro Sport. We paid for the scientist, sent it to test markets, boxed it, and branded it. We believed in the product and we were ready to launch. Suddenly a competitor started infringing on our trademark. I took a step back, looked at our resources, and asked some questions: Do I really want to risk launching this product and having to rebrand it later? Do I want to spend my time fighting over a brand that represents less than 1 percent of my revenue? On the other hand, after all this work, do I really want to pull the plug?

In the end we yanked the product, revamped the entire energy drink line, rebranded it, and by the time this book is on the shelves, the revenue lines for it will be far greater than 1 percent. We'll have much better results than we would have had if we'd continued down our path with the original strategy.

If you find yourself reading this and realizing that you may have taken the wrong approach to some of your own decisions, don't worry, because "sometimes the fastest way forward is to go backward." That's why the motto above my desk is "The path is all math." Don't get emotionally attached to projects. It's math, not emotion. As Steve Jobs said, "Focus is saying no." And that one principle has added more than $200 billion to Apple's market cap since he retook the company. And all too often we creative types like to say yes. The more things you say yes to or try to do, the less productive you are.

I have a mantra for my personal life and my companies: "*Focus should be a four-letter word.*" Try it and watch. When a person comes to me with a new idea and it's clearly not a priority, instead of dropping the f-bomb, I say to him or her, "What the focus are you talking about?" or "Go focus yourself."

Remember, entrepreneurship isn't about the size of your task list or how fast you can get through your inbox; it's about the things you need to do, and doing them well. At least it is if you want to be the kind of entrepreneur who makes an impact, and especially if you want to be the kind who makes money. If you have a thousand things on your list, how do you put a price tag on any of them? Only a few things are going to move the needle. Take no pride when you've done a hundred things, but none of them improved your bottom line.

If you were to take only one thing I tell you and apply it to your business and your life, apply these words: if you say yes to too many seemingly good ideas, then you have one bad idea of a company and a poor management culture. I've learned this lesson the hard way. I tried to do too much and, well, I did too much. I didn't focus on my company's core competencies or the largest value creator on the list, and it cost me millions, in cash and in lost opportunities.

In my entire career I've never looked back and thought I should have said yes to something. In fact, it's quite the opposite. My million-dollar mistakes, as you will find out, are rooted in not saying no often enough. An example is from 2008, just as the economy was melting down, when I had my company focused on launching twenty-some-odd products. At the peak of the failing economy, I was shoving new flavor mixers and holiday catalogues down people's throats when everyone else was worried about the future. And on top of everything, I was running Path-Connect at the same time. I was adding things to my plate when I should have been focusing on the most important thing: adapting to the economic shift. It's partly age and experience, but I run things much differently now.

Just say no—if the idea is good enough, it will come back.

The key is to be intimately involved with your business to the point where you understand its intricacies well enough to know what needs to happen immediately and what can wait, and to be detached enough to view the situation objectively so your decisions are not clouded by emotion.

Our business model is extremely complicated at ViSalus. We have customer/distributor ratios, legal costs, R&D, international shipping costs, a constantly growing compensation plan payout, capital needs, inventory, a supply chain—there are no less than sixty different variables on any given day that contribute to our business model, but only a few that drive it.

I once sat in a boardroom with Bob Goergen when the topic of expanding ViSalus into Europe was brought up. It's an intricate and expensive process at best, but I was all for it. I wanted to expand, and grow fast. I loved the idea of conquering the EU.

Bob said, "Ryan, this is what I like to call a 'bet the company' project." If it fails or you miss your window, you've risked your entire business. He was absolutely right; if we'd pushed for the expansion, we wouldn't be in business today. When the recession hit, it would have been right when I would have been on the ground trying to conquer the EU, as I lost the USA.

As a CEO, you need to be the foremost expert in the multiple variables that drive your business. Someone has to know the business so well that when you look at projects, you understand the impact each will have. And that person is you; no one else will have the same instincts.

## WATCH YOUR WALLET

All too often we assume as entrepreneurs that our employees are treating our money as though it were their own. Sometimes, of course, they don't. At SkyPipeline, one of my employees made an error with an account, and we lost a customer as a result. I took the employee aside and explained the lifetime value of the customer and how a careless error had cost us more than $100,000 in the long run. The employee had no idea that a thousand-dollar-per-month account was worth $100,000 to the company. Needless to say, he didn't make any more hundred-thousand-dollar errors. Your job as the CEO is to insist that the highest priority for each employee is to save you money, make you money, or both.

It's extremely helpful to ask your board of directors, other advisers, and employees to help prioritize the things that will keep your business growing and prospering. Sometimes they can see the forest through the trees when you can't.

But sometimes your employees won't save you a buck—or make you one, for that matter—because it might mean extra work. In previous companies there have been days when I've approached my management team with a project I believed in and been met with subtle resistance. And I've been left wondering, is it because they don't agree with the value of the project? In reality, the reason they resisted the idea was because nobody wanted to do more work. They were thinking, this is going to take my entire weekend. And they started stalling, or persuading others not to do it.

When this is the case, start by reminding the team of the company's priorities; if they persist, a simple reprimand is in order. And if they continue, then you have to fire the employees, because plain and simply, they don't have the priorities of the company at heart. It's one of my Golden Rules that compensation drives behavior and sometimes the threat of losing compensation will drive people to action. Conversely, if employees discover ways to save money or make money, they deserve compensation even if it's in the form of recognition as simple as a public thank-you.

In the early days of ViSalus, we had a hiccup in our computer system on a day when we wrote and sent out a commission check in the amount of $70,000. There was a computer error again the next day—the computer was saying that the check hadn't gone out—so one of our staff members sent out another $70,000. Two checks to the same people for a total of $140,000!

By the time we caught it, the checks had been cashed. The people on the other end must have said, "Great, they sent us two checks!" The excuse was that it was a computer system error. That's a wonderful excuse, and a legitimate one, but if you own the company and you're funding it, you would have to put an additional $70,000 into your business because of a system error. Someone might just as well have stolen $70,000 out of your wallet.

There are no excuses for that type of error. You have to watch every check that goes in and out of your business. You must put controls in place to ensure that money isn't running out the back door while you're trying so hard to bring it in through the front. I've known countless entrepreneurs who have had their money accidentally lost, deliberately embezzled, or incompetently spent on idiotic things because they weren't paying attention to their wallets when other people had access to them.

So to recap, don't lose sight of the principles by which you created the company, and don't let the details of running it tear your focus from the big picture. Obsessing over things is good when it comes to solving high-priority problems one by one. With each step, make sure that your people are right behind you. And when the ideas they bring to you are out of line? Just say no! I've scrapped projects so often that I could have filled a landfill with the collateral damage. I don't regret a single time I've said no. My point is, watch your wallet, be just as proud of what you do as what you don't do, and focus on first things first.

# 9

# WHAT'S DRIVING YOU?

The Death Cycle: Day in and day out, you get up before dawn to make a grueling commute to a dingy building, where you spend eight, nine, or ten hours a day working at a job that doesn't fulfill you, doesn't exhibit your talents, and makes you dread each moment you have to spend thinking about it. By the time you get home to your family, you are too drained to enjoy their company and too tired from thinking of the day of drudgery ahead to make the most of your free time.

How do you break out of it? The first step is to figure out what motivates you.

Motivation can steer both our short-term and long-term decision making. It can affect our personality, temperament, and interests. It is one of the most powerful forces in our lives—and it is often subconscious. We rarely stop to question exactly what our motivation is in each circumstance, but by taking stock of the motives behind our decisions, each subsequent move will be more deliberate, directed, and effective.

The very first step in creating your business is rooted in motivation— what drives you to want to become an entrepreneur? "I lost my job and I need something to do" isn't going to cut it. A mind-set that allows something external to be in control also allows your circumstances to define you. And we are not defined wholly by our circumstances, because if that were the case, I would still be in jail.

In my experience, there are four main drivers that urge an individual toward becoming an entrepreneur: independence, wealth, recognition and fame, and contribution. You will likely find that you have a mixture of all of them, but it is important that you pinpoint the main driver by figuring out how far you would be willing to go to obtain each one. When you discover which of the four you would pursue with more intensity and determination than you would the others, you've found your primary driver.

Independence is a common driving factor for many entrepreneurs. They are motivated by the day when they can fire their boss and walk out of the office with confidence. If setting your own terms of employment and working by your own standards toward your goals sounds appealing, then independence is probably your main driver—and that's one of the most exciting things about entrepreneurship.

Being one's own boss is a strong motivator for many people. A thriving, free-market capitalist system in which anyone can try to succeed by doing what he or she loves is one of the aspects of the American tradition that makes this country great; independence is an integral part of that tradition.

Wealth is also a great motivator. Unless you were lucky enough to be born as a trust-fund baby, chances are good that you have to work for a living. There is more to being driven by wealth than simply wanting a fat paycheck, however; if that's all you're after, then obviously there are far more secure means of achieving that goal.

There is no need to be ashamed if wealth is your driver. It has been the driver of nearly every great advancement that's ever been made throughout history.

Some people act as if *profit* is a dirty word, as if the pursuit of making money as a small-business owner somehow makes you greedy, or that concern with the bottom line means you're obsessed with money.

Nothing could be further from the truth. By generating wealth, you are providing for your own needs, for your family's needs, and—moving beyond your own immediate considerations—probably creating jobs in your community as well.

Recognition and fame are also legitimate reasons why some people enter the entrepreneurial life. If you have a solid product or service, you should take pride in that, and having your name associated with what you do demonstrates to your customers (and your employees) that you have confidence in your company.

Fame can be a great motivator for someone who is tired of being counted as only a number in a company. The desire to have your skills noticed can be a strong motivation, especially if you have felt underappreciated in your previous job. Recognition might be as simple as proving to the world that you are savvy and tough enough to succeed as a business owner.

Everyone wants his or her fifteen minutes, and fame can make you money. It can make life easier, but can also swing like a double-edged sword. There's an old saying about recognition: "Babies cry for it, grown men die for it."

Contribution is also an important driver. People who desire a sense of contribution feel compelled to give back to their community or to meet a basic need for people, animals, or the environment—any cause that promises to enrich lives or leave the world a better place.

Often, entrepreneurially minded individuals who find themselves driven to contribute are drawn to the service industry or nonprofits. If this is you, you may find yourself in a bit of a quandary: Is it possible to operate a for-profit business like a nonprofit one or vice versa? Absolutely. Someone's profits fund nonprofits.

True nonprofits depend largely upon grants, donations, and public funding to operate. You can create a business model that meets the same needs as a traditional nonprofit, but you can operate in such a way that it is not dependent on external funding. A business that works with local governments to help place people in jobs or develop work skills can be self-supporting through the city's or county's payment for services. For instance, it is entirely possible to run a profitable business dedicated to helping other local businesses go green.

Do not let the drive to be a social contributor scare you away from the prospect of starting your own business. The two certainly can coexist. Just recognize that your ultimate goals are probably going to be different from those of many of the other business owners in your area. That's simply because you have different drivers, and the drive to contribute can be the foundation of a financially successful business whose profits can be further invested in the community, doing even more good work. For example, at ViSalus, our Feed the Kids initiative is a for-profit business model that serves nonprofits.

Did any of these four drivers strike a chord with you? Keep in mind that your primary driver might change with time and circumstance. Personally, I've felt each one become my primary motivation at different points in my life. The key is recognizing where you are right now as you get ready to start building your business plan and making sure that you are honest in your assessment of yourself. Otherwise, your business and your life will arrive in the wrong place because the goal you pursued the most aggressively wasn't the one you really wanted.

If you are driven by fame, you may find that the desire to amass personal wealth has to become secondary as you take on gratis projects to get your name out there. If you are driven by independence, you may have to wait until you have a slightly higher bank balance before you begin investing in charitable or socially conscious causes, simply because you are pursuing security first. But later, when your business is firmly established and you're ready to move to a new challenge, you might find your primary driver moving, too.

By determining the driver that best fits your current situation and mind-set, you will be articulating authority over your circumstances. You are giving a label to the personal force that is bringing about this change in your life.

As we all know, there are a number of things that go into becoming successful and maintaining success. Additionally, the mark of having "arrived" can be different for each person. The point at which you feel you have made it is a very personal thing. But by staying mindful of the criteria by which you set your goals, you'll have a better sense of how to evaluate your progress as you move your business forward.

My advice is to be aware of your primary motivation. For me, as I got ready to launch my first venture, the driver was pretty simple: I was a fame-and-recognition guy. A guy that I had worked with at Logix had become a multimillionaire entrepreneur; he was driving a Ferrari; all my friends were talking about him; and he was all over the news. I'm competitive. And I wanted to compete.

The next question you need to consider in creating your business plan is this: Where is your passion? What do you absolutely love doing? After identifying your motivation, this needs to be the next starting point for developing your company, because if your heart isn't in it, you'll have a much more difficult time finding the energy required to get your idea off the ground and running.

Take stock of your skills, interests, and hobbies. Do you find a common thread? Determine what you are naturally drawn to, and evaluate your strengths, whether or not you have formal training in the area. Do not be afraid to push around some of the boundaries and preconceived ideas that might be limiting how you view yourself and your talents.

For example, a friend was starting to question the future of her career. She was a successful actress and model who had appeared in several movies. She had a definite career established, but she didn't love it.

We discussed the importance of finding her driver—identifying the appeal of that one thing that would motivate her to go to all ends. It wasn't recognition. There are quick and easy ways to gain fame (especially in the world that is Hollywood) that she was not willing to pursue. It wasn't wealth. There were other profitable lines of work, but she was focused more on obtaining personal fulfillment and expression than on chasing a big paycheck.

So I asked her a very basic question: What would you choose as a career if you were guaranteed a steady income for the rest of your life, provided that you pursued this one thing? She immediately answered that she would be an interior designer. She loved color, shape, texture, and lines—this was why she was drawn to modeling in the first place. She had a strong sense of the aesthetic and of what makes something visually appealing. She'd never been to design school, but she always found herself mentally arranging and rearranging interiors because of an innate artistic sense.

However, she'd always had a strict definition of what *artist* meant: palette and canvas or clay and wheel. She didn't realize that her own interest in expression also made her an artist. To watch her start to redefine herself in those terms was exciting. She had an end in mind, which was to create beauty to make an impact on people through interior environment. Her vehicle could change from photography to acting to design, but what she was seeking was the same: she wanted to obtain fulfillment from design by asserting creative control over artistic drive.

The first home she designed was mine, and that led to several other clients. Now she's well on her way to a new career where she does what she loves.

## YOU'RE NOT A STEREOTYPE

That's how the human mind works—we create definitions and an identity for ourselves, and we don't always realize that we can shift and apply our experience to new industries and new ideas. People who come from an industry rarely change it. Jeff Bezos of Amazon.com never sold books; Steve Jobs never sold music. The Model T was invented by a two-time businessman failure, with a background in farming. And he was Henry Ford. A very antisocial guy created tools that enabled him to be more social, and shifted the way 600 million people communicate. Zuckerberg didn't say, "I'm not social." He said, "How do I shift humanity to *my way* of being social?"

For me, the area that really sparked my interest was technology, but my passion for that field was multifaceted. I was driven by intellectual curiosity for the subject matter; however, I was also intrigued by its earning potential and by the fulfillment and reward that it brought to me as an outlet for creativity.

My life and my entry into computer science were anything but stereotypical. My first experience with computers was fueled by my troubled relationship with my father. Early in middle school, when my dad's addictions were the worst and I was still living at home, I earned some terrible grades in school.

Rather than face the beating I knew was coming, I watched the mailbox and pounced on the report card when it arrived. I knew that Dad wouldn't miss it by a day or two, so I went over to my neighbor Jeremy's house and asked to use his family's new computer. I spent a couple of days carefully recalculating my GPA—if a D changed to a B+, how would that change the numbers?—and counting every space and hard return line so that my fake report card would be identical to the real one. Methodically and precisely, we re-created that report card on the dot matrix printer, with better (but believable) grades. I had steamed the envelope open, so when the new report card was ready, I dropped it back in, glued the envelope carefully shut, and put it back in the mailbox. My parents never caught on, and I avoided another pounding.

I realize that perhaps this is not the best story to introduce how I discovered my passion. But it's honest—and I still have that report card. More than just putting one over on my dad, though, that incident stayed with me for a long time because it was empowering. I felt that a computer gave me the opportunity to assert control over a bad situation.

From that point on, I'd watch my sister's dad, Steve (we all have different parents), repair computers, which he did for a living, and I was captivated by the engineering of them. I was fascinated by movies like *War Games,* which showed how kids could hack other computers. That association stuck with me: computers equal power.

Later, when I was actively a juvenile delinquent, I got into shoplifting. I didn't steal normal things like candy or video games; I went into computer stores and "liberated" books on how to repair and program computers. I read up on everything I could about the technical side of computers because it was empowering.

One day when I was in Juvenile Hall (for the aforementioned shoplifting, among other things), I was sent into the computer room for a typing class. I realized quickly that I was one of the only people there who knew how to manipulate the computer system. From then on, every time I was in the computer room, I would mess with the system. Sometimes I would shut it down or delete a few files because the prompts were so simple back then. Sometimes I was even asked by an oblivious instructor to fix the "problem" that was making the computers crash. It was such a thrill for me to have control of their network while they controlled me.

I talked about computers all the time, to the point that the first gift Robert Hunt (soon to be my stepfather) gave me was a CD-ROM. It was his birthday gift to me because his computer was pretty old and slow, and with the way I constantly talked about programming, he figured I'd want something I could use to maximize the performance of that antiquated system. It was from this background that I started eyeing the data center at Logix, which was my first real opportunity in the field of computers, and that allowed me to start climbing the ranks.

The first time I boarded a plane in my adult life was for a trip from Los Angeles to Minneapolis to discuss a piece of software that Logix was developing for the Mystic Lake Casino Hotel. I was twenty years old and had limited real-world experience, but as I talked to the president and other executives at Mystic Lake about what we could do for them that our competitors weren't doing, I had a realization: I wasn't the guy getting the commission for the sale, but I was the guy they bought the software from and someone else got credit even though I had to build it.

It was suddenly so clear. Not only did I realize that an obvious passion for my business helped close the sale, but beyond that, I recognized that I was the engineer behind the product. I could write the code, or I could oversee the code writing; I could do the sales, or I could manage the account. And that was when I knew that I wanted to be an entrepreneur. It was from that aha! moment that I started to formulate my business plan for 24/7 Tech, a twenty-four-hour-a-day technical support service—my first business.

Our drivers and passions can come from wildly different sources; the key is to understand what they are and why.

I had a bit of a rockier path. Even when I was striving to avoid detection, be it faking that report card or "fixing" the computers in juvenile detention, I was still seeking recognition. That was my driver. I wanted the satisfaction of knowing that I had mastered a skill, and (as I started to realize later, while working for my stepfather) I wanted someone to take notice of that and be proud of me. As that recognition started to pour in, my own confidence in the field grew to the point where I knew I would be able to branch out on my own in the field that I found most amplified my driver.

Think about Anthony Hopkins's road to success. Before he was an established superstar, he acted in every production he could. He was onstage as much as possible, and often for no pay, but he was driven by the love for what he did, and he was willing to sacrifice almost anything to pursue it. What would you go to any ends to pursue, as Anthony Hopkins did with acting? What grabs your interest and won't let go, despite the long hours, low pay, and constant obstacles in your path? What wakes you up at night and keeps you from going back to sleep because you can't stop thinking about it?

It comes back to the question with which we began: What do you desire most? Independence, wealth, recognition and fame, or a feeling of contribution? Which one would you sacrifice the most to obtain?

Write down your interests, your skills, and do some soul searching. Think about it. Talk to your friends and family and ask them what they think your main driver is out of the four. See what they reply. Sometimes it's easier for others to see what your driver is, because as an entrepreneur, you've got to have a little bit of all of them.

Listen to your friends and family. But in the end, you have to trust your gut. Don't go with what sounds like the right answer or what you think other people expect of you. Know your motivation, choose a business you would do without pay and build something that wakes you up in the middle of the night, something that you're proud of and you can't stop thinking about. Like Jay-Z said, "You're not a businessman; you're a business, man."

# 10

## TAP THOSE ASSETS

---

Every one of us has untapped, undiscovered, and unmonetized assets. I've laid out some examples in this chapter in hopes that they will give you a solid base to start your own inventory and spark ideas about assets you might not have previously considered.

In his book *Outliers*, Malcolm Gladwell makes the point that it takes approximately ten thousand hours of training and practice to truly master a skill set at a professional level. Sometimes you've put your ten thousand hours in and you don't even know it. Make sure you take into account any related experience in your area of interest, and remember, you don't necessarily need to have a degree or extensive formal classroom training to succeed. If you need ten thousand hours of experience, then time is your greatest asset, so how are you investing it? Most employees work 40 hours a week, but in my opinion, they aren't really applying all those hours to perfecting their business skills. Many of those hours are wasted talking around the coffeepot, on Facebook, or on other unproductive activities. If half of your yearly 2,083 hours was really applied toward building your business, at that rate it would take you about ten years to become a professional entrepreneur.

Take a look at your network, since this is also an asset. Take stock of the most powerful and well-connected people in your circle. Make a list of individuals you can reach out to, and keep those connections hot with the occasional note or follow-up e-mail. Don't go overboard, but keep yourself in their mind. As you'll see later in the chapter, these connections can be the most valuable assets in your arsenal.

When I add a person to my network, I always start thinking about potential partnerships or business ventures. If someone in your network already owns a business, then you might be able to create a product or service that complements and leverages that individual's customer base.

Also, how are you being perceived by the people in your network? If they see you as an amazing writer because of your candid and funny e-mails, you could start a business as a freelance writer. The landscaping around your house might be so meticulous and beautiful that many of your friends would hire you to do the same for them.

Other untapped assets might lie in your affiliations with reputable people and organizations. For instance, when I started real estate investing, I leveraged my stepfather's name and volume in real estate to my benefit when buying homes and making investments. Who in your family and group of friends has a reputation that you might be able to leverage in your new business?

Get creative. When it comes to leveraging the assets in your network, many times having access is better than owning. For instance, I have a friend who owns a private jet. Now the maintenance fees, fuel, and the cost of upkeep is astronomical for a private jet, but when I want to use his jet, he simply charges me what it costs him. I can put eight employees on a jet from Los Angeles to Las Vegas, and it costs me far less than it would if I travel via commercial airline and it saves me a lot of time.

Also, location is an asset. For instance, if you live in Silicon Valley, your access to high-tech companies is unparalleled in the world. Or inversely, if you're creating an event planning service, the small community you live in might be better because families tend to gather more frequently.

You should also consider whether there are any niches to fill. If you can identify a definite need for the area your business is in—there is no fabric or craft supply store within thirty miles, for example—you can have a clearer sense of how to tailor your plan to fill that hole. Or maybe there's already a business in place that fills that niche, but it's currently up for sale.

The best example I can offer from my own life comes from one of my earliest business ventures. One of my sisters was married to a man who owned a small Internet service provider that served their community. It was 2001, and there was a mix of nervousness from the dot-com bubble's recent implosion and optimism that the Internet was still a solid and reliable resource.

My brother-in-law got word of another small Internet company called SkyPipeline, which was coming up for sale. It was struggling, but because it was based in populous Santa Barbara, I could see right away that there was a definite opportunity for expansion, and the course of action I could take to turn it around.

It was a tiny company, started with only about $20,000 in capital, and it served fewer than ten customers. Of course, you have to start somewhere with building your client base, but they were making less than $1,000 per month and were burning far more trying to provide service.

I still owned 24/7 Tech, my technical support company, but I felt that this struggling little wireless company would be a great investment as a side business, and could even grow into my primary focus.

The point is, it may be that your best opportunity is to create an entirely new business, but entrepreneurship is not necessarily creating a business from the ground up. There may be small companies out there that are ripe for purchase, restructuring, and rebranding. Keep your eyes open.

Around the same time that I was looking at SkyPipeline, I was slated to make a presentation to a potential 24/7 Tech investor. King Lee was the ex-CEO of Quarterdeck, a large software company whose products we used daily. I knew he was a well-connected individual, and I persuaded him to meet with me so I could pitch my business idea. At the end of my presentation, he remarked frankly, "Ryan, this thing that you were telling me about with wireless service—that has legs. Everything else I've heard I'm not interested in. Let me know if you ever decide to do the wireless thing."

That was the signal I needed to go forward with SkyPipeline. I knew that I would have one interested party once the new company was up and running. But how could I get to that point? I found out that raising capital was far more difficult than I had imagined. Time and again I was rejected by venture capitalists I spoke with because they didn't think it was a scalable model, or they felt there were too many competitors in the market, or they just didn't think it was a good business to invest in because it was already struggling. I believed in my vision for SkyPipeline, though, so I decided to pursue one other direction that had worked so far: I networked.

I knew of a successful angel investor in Santa Barbara named Pete Sutherland, who I thought might be interested in the potential of the company. I was able to book a meeting with Pete to present him with my idea for purchasing SkyPipeline, a plan that involved selling my share of 24/7 Tech. Pete was willing to help fund my business plan and to let me work with some accountants to get my finances in order, partly because I had demonstrated a willingness to reach out to other people for effective fund-raising, and partly because I was investing a huge portion of myself into the project. Pete's assistance enabled me to go forward with the purchase and helped the business grow rapidly once I took over.

My investment in 24/7 Tech was small—not much more than about $30,000—and combined with my savings, I was able to scrape together $20,000 to make an offer on SkyPipeline. Of course I acted as if I had all the confidence and assets in the world, but writing out that check really hurt me because I knew I had a mortgage and a car payment, and it was really a leap of faith. I was going all in.

But where networking really made a difference for me was when Pete stepped in and was willing to mentor me, to talk me through the negotiating process. Even though I started out with no office, employees, or fancy logo, I had a solid plan and obvious confidence in myself and in the telecom business, and those assets convinced others it was a solid investment. Pete explained to me that this ability to network was one of the most crucial elements in success. Business veterans already know that fact, but as a new kid starting out, this was an important lesson for me. And it paid off. Pete agreed to invest $75,000 to help get SkyPipeline off the ground, and then he agreed to help me lead a round of financing with other investors. And it was all because he saw that I was willing to reach out and do the legwork to meet people, make connections, and gain interest.

I bought SkyPipeline in July 2001 and immediately started meeting with potential investors and clients to whom Pete had introduced me. With $75,000 in the bank—the first half of his investment money—I already had my eye on a bigger goal to expand the company right away.

And then September 11 happened.

That summer the Dow had reached its all-time high. The NASDAQ had also been doing extremely well and was just starting to slow. But after the terrorist attacks, the market plummeted and investors lost fortunes. Here I was, one month into a business, and the market was the most volatile it had been in my lifetime. All my potential investors pulled out for more secure investments, nervous that telecom was too edgy.

I knew it was necessary to put Pete's influence to work or risk total failure. I called him up and explained that if we couldn't get any more backers—and soon—he'd lose the $75,000 he'd already put into the business. A smart man and a shrewd investor, he went to work with me, reaching out to various people and companies to give our sales pitch. By December of that same year, we'd closed $415,000 worth of financing, and the company had an exponentially larger clientele than when I'd started. Networking and influence can be very, very powerful tools.

I learned that lesson again as we moved forward into 2002, when I got a call from a man named Fred Warren, who had a ranch in the Santa Ynez Valley, not far from Michael Jackson's Neverland estate. It was a rural area with thousands of acres of open land, but it was also a community with a lot of wealth. Fred wanted our service, and because my company was operating in the area, he gave me a call to see if SkyPipeline could handle the job.

Of course I was willing to take any contract I could, but I also realized that the cost of providing service just to Fred's ranch was probably not going to be a wise move financially speaking.

I had no idea who this individual was, but he said he'd be willing to pay the $5,000 required to set up a tower facing his property, so I offered to meet with him to discuss the details and tell him more about our company—to see if it was an arrangement we could both benefit from. In the meantime, I Googled him and learned that he was the founder of Brentwood Associates—and one of the world's most-successful venture capitalists.

We sat down at our meeting, and I pitched my business to him, explaining about the funding I did have and the potential investors I had lined up. Fred looked at me and said, "You need more than another $415,000. You need another million, and I'd like to participate with you." Suddenly, I had a new business partner with more influence, clout, and capital than I could have ever imagined.

Now, obviously, an experience like the one I just described is atypical. But it doesn't change the fact that a few well-situated investors can give your business a huge advantage—especially in its early stages. Also, don't be afraid to ask one of the mentors with whom you have had personal contact whether he or she would be willing to be listed as a reference for you. Hand in hand with networking and mentorship, your references are assets. A solid set of references from well-respected individuals can create a sense of stability and legitimacy with prospective investors and clients.

Also, sometimes trash can be an asset. To use SkyPipeline as an example again, when Global Crossing was shutting down, it was going to cost them a significant amount of money to remove all their antennas from the coast of California. I was able to relieve them of that burden by putting their antenna towers to good use with my company SkyPipeline and, as a result, I was able to leverage $50,000,000 of their assets. One man's trash is another man's treasure.

I hope I've given you some good ideas so far. When taking stock of your own asset inventory, you'll need to strike a balance between being realistic and allowing yourself to think big. As you make your lists, it will be helpful to create a kind of ranking system to rate how certain or secure an asset is. For example, if you have $15,000 in the bank but anticipate that you might be able to secure a $20,000 small-business loan, make a note of that. Both are assets, but one is certain and the other is a realistic —but as of yet, unattained—goal. The most important thing is that you are thorough, organized, and honest with yourself as you go through this self-audit.

Of course, if you have money in the bank, that's the best asset to start with, but even now that I *have* money, I still prefer using other people's money in building my businesses. As an entrepreneur, you're constantly taking all the risk, but when you bring in investors, it spreads the risk and brings complementary talents, skills, and experience to the table. In chapter 16, "Raising Money," I'll teach you how to hold on to as many of your own assets as possible, by tapping other people's assets, too.

# 11

## RISK AND SACRIFICE

---

The prospect of starting your own business sounds exciting, promising, and liberating—you're eager to get started. Now is the point where you've got to start considering the less glamorous side of entrepreneurship. You need to determine how averse you are to risk.

Some people thrive on the thrill ride of risk; some people collapse under the strain of it. Others neither relish it nor shrink from it, but simply accept it as a necessary part of their business plan. Which type of person are you?

The fact of the matter is entrepreneurship isn't for everyone. It is necessary to have a firm grasp on your tolerance for risk before you can even hope to make a jump into this business. Your ability to manage living on the edge financially for at least a year is, in many ways, what will make or break your business.

How far are you willing to go and what are you willing to lose to own your own business? It's not so much a question of strength, as it is a question of temperament. Is your personality one that can adequately deal with the various unpredictable and constantly changing unknowns that go along with business ownership?

In our last chapter we discussed the need to define your assets. Now, you've got to assess your tolerance for risk—and the tolerance of others around you.

Any commercial you see on TV or any claim you hear from someone making the pitch that "I made X dollars in my very first month working from home!" is likely a gross exaggeration, or the person's testimony was derived from significant skill and relevant experience. Security is not going to be part of the game for quite some time. Are you ready and willing to deal with that?

You've got to be frank about who you really are and not just who you want to be, or how you want to be seen by others. It's a good thing to show a lot of confidence and toughness when you're meeting with potential investors, but when you're considering whether this world is right for you, you can't put on a show for yourself.

It's really not about strong versus weak, or tough versus soft. This is about the way you look at the world and the way that your body and mind process stressful situations. If you know that you are not someone who performs well in high-pressure situations, you need to seriously question whether entrepreneurship is the right move for you.

First, you'll need to consider what is at risk. Your personal finances will definitely be at risk because you'll be investing a large amount of those into starting your business. Your home or car may be at risk if you use them as collateral for a bank loan. Your luxury items, such as a boat, might be at risk if you find you need to sell them to raise capital. Your lifestyle will certainly be at risk as you make sacrifices.

But there is more at risk than just your material possessions. Your sense of security will be at risk as you wait for deals to go through. Your peace of mind will be at risk as you're stressed about establishing a clientele or securing enough investors to grow the company to keep up with the market. And, of course, if it all falls through, you risk the disappointment and heartache of a failed business.

It's essential to remember, however, that risk taking is not the same as being reckless. You may be someone who tends to be fairly cautious in your decisions and conservative with your plans. That doesn't mean you're not equipped to handle the pressures of entrepreneurship. In fact, you might be ideally suited for it.

People often confuse high-risk tolerance with a willingness to fly off the handle with spur-of-the-moment choices that reflect little market research and no serious consideration for the current situation of the company. They are not the same thing at all. Reckless people rarely succeed in this field because they don't properly invest the time and energy required to make informed decisions, risky though the decisions might be.

If you are someone who craves risk for the sake of an adrenaline rush, go skydiving. If you're someone who can put up with risk as the cost of doing business, then start a company.

Consider each of the following situations:

1. You have enough to take care of three months' worth of expenses in the bank, but no more. Sales have dried up and it looks as if you'll barely be able to cover operating expenses this month. Can you handle it?
2. Your bank account has reached zero. You have some leads but no signed deals, and the end of the month is rapidly approaching. Can you handle it?
3. Your balance is overdrawn, the credit card companies are calling you demanding payment, your child has to have her tonsils out, the transmission just blew on your family's only car, five customers are clamoring for service on their accounts, and your last investment pitch was just soundly rejected. Can you handle it?

At what point would you curl up into a ball on the floor? Which scenario would be the one where you would finally decide it was all too much for you? Where is the line where you just couldn't find it within yourself to pick up the phone one more time and start working your way down a list of prospective clients?

There are degrees of discomfort, and everyone has a different breaking point. But if you want to be an entrepreneur, there is no choice. You always have to be willing to make that next call, go present that next pitch, and work to close that next deal. If you know that you've got it in you to go out and sell, even in the toughest of circumstances, then you've probably got the right personality, temperament, mind-set, and confidence to make it as a business owner. If not, you may want to reconsider your decision, or at least your approach.

There are an unlimited number of entrances into the world of entrepreneurship—you don't have to jump into it immediately, or even all at once. Some people can't sleep at night without knowing that they have six months of living expenses in the bank. This is admirable and responsible. However, if this is your comfort level, you might not be ready to become an entrepreneur. You should start saving money now to have that security cushion, with the goal that in two years you'll be ready to strike out on your own. You may even want to take on a second job during this time frame, knowing that the extra income is going to support your goals of business ownership and that the current sacrifice will lessen the risk to some extent.

It might be better, too, for you to keep two accounts during those twelve months—one for living expenses once you start your own business, and one for your business fund. If you know that you tend to be a more cautious and risk-averse individual, then you'll probably want to make sure that you've got a solid savings account not only for your family but also to have a nice chunk of change for launching your business when the time is right. It can take quite a while to get the right investors interested when you're first starting out, so having in place several months of the initial start-up cost will be really important for your peace of mind.

Maybe during this time you can begin to acquire the necessary equipment, establish your Web site, or research the necessary paperwork and tax laws regarding the kind of company you'd like to establish. By taking these small but essential steps, you can help to spread out the cost and the legwork over a longer stretch of time so that the impact isn't quite so jarring and the financial burden of the start-up cost doesn't hit you all at once.

The same thing is true if you're someone who is not comfortable with owing large amounts of money. Though they are a great tool for a lot of people, small-business loans might not be the best route for you because of the looming knowledge that payments are going to come due and interest will be accruing. If that's how you feel about the matter, that's great—it's healthy to want to live debt-free. Unfortunately, that's not an option for most first-time entrepreneurs.

When I started SkyPipeline I had to put a lot of expenses on my credit cards. I personally guaranteed hundreds of thousands of dollars in loans and had to live off the company. This technique for starting a business is called bootstrapping. I remember saying to myself, "If this doesn't work, I'm ruined." Leveraging yourself as I did is not for the security-driven, employee-minded person. I recall having to make several difficult personal decisions in order to keep the business alive. I can look back now and say it was all worth it; however, I will never forget the feeling of financial uncertainty that haunted me along the way. My advice to all entrepreneurs is to try to avoid personal guarantees. I've learned this lesson the hard way.

In the end, though, you need to be aware that nothing will ever remove all the risk. No amount of preparation—personal, financial, or otherwise—will completely lift the uncertainty that surrounds business ownership. There is no fail-safe approach to being an entrepreneur, which is why it is so important to do this self-assessment before you get into the thick of things.

The most important thing is that you know what you're getting into. I've been in scenarios just like those listed above. Each is scary in its own way, but you have to know how far you can go before you break.

The other thing you have to consider is what the risk tolerance is of the other people in your life. Who else is depending on you, and how much risk can *they* tolerate?

What other needs exist in your life right now? If you're married, what is your spouse's employment situation? Will he or she be starting this business alongside you or working at another job that will be supplying income as you pursue your own business? Do you have any children who will be getting ready to head off to college soon or who may have special needs? And what about elderly parents either within your household or in assisted living—do you provide any support for them? Will you be needing to in the next few years?

If you feel confident that you can take on a business, where is your partner's breaking point? At what point will your spouse decide he or she can't live with the uncertainty and the sacrifice anymore? You may be able to weather the storm, but if your partner can't—if your partner craves security over any of the entrepreneurial drivers of independence, wealth, recognition and fame, or contribution—then you may need to rethink your plan.

Perhaps you can agree to a prearranged stopping point when you will both decide that enough is enough. You may be considering this business move in order to provide your family with a better life, which is totally admirable. If you are lucky and your family is fully supportive of the risk, you're going to be starting out in a great position with a solid support system in place. But if they aren't on board with your plan and don't share the same level of risk tolerance as you, your work on their behalf may all be in vain.

I'm not giving empty warnings; I know firsthand that this can happen, because I have lost a few relationships over this same issue. You have to make sure your family is supportive of the work you are doing and the lengths to which you have to go in order to get your company on its feet. Otherwise, the discord that can result is a risk you'll have to consider as well. That's the only relationship advice I will give; I'm no expert on the subject, but I can tell you to make sure the person you're with can handle your career and its high risk.

There is a risk in making the move to start your own business, but there is also a risk in not acting. Don't let fear stop you from doing what you feel driven to do.

Martin Luther King Jr. once revived a quote from Benjamin Franklin, who said, "Most men die at 21; we just don't bury them until they're 60 or 70." Don't be someone who lives a life of excuses instead of action.

## GET REALLY UNCOMFORTABLE

Closely related to your tolerance for risk is your willingness to sacrifice. You need to be able to stomach a large amount of uncertainty in your daily life, and you need to be willing to pare down to a minimal existence for as long as it takes to reach a point of sustainability in your company, which means at the very least a year or more. You have to determine just how uncomfortable you can stand to be, forfeiting not only luxury items or small indulgences, but also forgoing your physical comfort. You need to consider this seriously because without a willingness to sacrifice, you are never going to achieve your business goals.

*Sacrifice* is a word we tend to hear a lot about from politicians, but it's not something most of us keep in the forefront of our minds every day. However, that is going to change when you enter the world of entrepreneurship. *Sacrifice* is going to be echoing in your head constantly as you make decisions about what you can afford, what you need, and what you're going to have to plan for.

There are several steps of sacrifice you'll have to take even before you formulate your business plan, starting with how you think about money in your personal life.

I think most middle-class Americans are in a holding pattern of comfort. They have a desire to keep up appearances, and then those appearances take on such a semblance of reality that the people living them believe they have to borrow money to maintain a lifestyle that was phony in the first place.

When I was growing up in Southern California, wealth was all around me. Even while living as a normal middle-class kid until the age of thirteen and then as a poor street kid for several years after that, I saw how the most successful business people, investors, and other professionals lived. Their lifestyle was what I wanted, and I was always curious about what it would take to get from where I was to where they were. What was different about the way they thought that opened them up to such success?

By the time I was in my early twenties and was back in the middle class, I had established a pattern of living that seemed very different from my neighbors. Whenever one of them earned a large amount of money, a new car or a new boat would inevitably show up in the driveway. Maybe a woman would be flashing some new jewelry or a man would be sporting a Rolex.

I fell into that trap more than once myself, purchasing a flashy new car that would stretch my budget or taking a lavish vacation with my raise or bonus. It feels good to spend money—I would feel like I had finally attained the standard of living I'd always wanted . . . until the bill came due. And then I realized the biggest difference between me and those people I had wanted so badly to emulate: they could afford to live in the manner I was only pretending to. And why could they afford it? Because they had been smart with their funds early on and could now reap the benefits.

Once I understood that difference, I quickly realized that my money would go a lot—*a lot*—further if I reinvested it instead of spending it. Once I started to channel money away from personal comfort items or status-driven indulgences and toward more entrepreneurial investments, I found that the returns would almost always generate even more capital. At first I spent the money expanding my business. Later I was able to use it to invest in other promising companies. And as the luxury brand items were depreciating in my neighbors' driveways or closets, my money was continuing to grow. Investment over consumption—that has to be an entrepreneur's mantra.

There is nothing wrong with spending your own hard-earned money in whatever way you see fit. My stepfather always told me to take 5 percent of my gains and reward myself, but that was it! When you start making millions a year, you can have a lot of fun with 5 percent. I am a great proponent of incentive and rewards programs. However, the long-term future of our money depends on the choices we make for it today. Do you want to have a business that is stable, a community fixture, and able to weather the markets? Do you want to reach a point when, maybe someday, you could maintain a comfortable lifestyle simply from the interest paid from your capital? Then you need to be willing to make sacrifices now.

Don't fall into the unhealthy pattern of continuously chasing the next cheapest offer for money from banks or credit card companies. That's how people land in debt, bankruptcy court, and in the cycle of miserable employment. The entrepreneurial road is continuously obstructed by the chase for cash. If your debt-to-income ratio is too high, you will never be able to launch your own business because the security of a secure income will keep you tied to your current position (if you are still employed), even if the work is mind-numbing. If you are currently out of work or anticipate being there soon, the same is true. If you are locked into debt and financing beyond your means, you will be desperate to take the first job that comes your way simply to be able to make your minimal payments. If you're in a hole, quit digging and do what you truly desire.

If you are part of the "comfort chase," as I like to call it, you have to start changing your mode of thinking long before you can hope to launch a feasible business. You have to think of your money as a tool for investment that is continuously working to bring you a return and build wealth rather than as a tool for buying you luxury items that only make it *appear* as if you are wealthy.

Remember that each time you decide not to spend, each time you choose not to pursue a new line of credit, you are investing in your future security and the security of your business. The point of investment, after all, is to sacrifice with a bit of risk in the present in order to return dividends in the future.

If you really love what you want to pursue, necessary sacrifices will be much easier to deal with, which is why it is so important to have your driver and passion clearly identified before you start pursuing your dream.

But the fact is, the business world is built on more than just dreams. It's built on hard numbers and profit margins. And that's where the second level of sacrifice comes in. Once you have made the necessary changes to your way of thinking about money *before* your entrepreneurial leap, you have to be willing to maintain those changes—and possibly even take them to a new level—once your plans get rolling.

When you have external investors in your company, you have a duty to make them a return. An investor might say, "All right, you told me what you love and how you propose to build a business around that. But what I want to know is how are you going to fund this business to support yourself and your lifestyle?" If you haven't considered the way you're going to live while getting your business off the ground, an investor is not going to be interested in anything else you have to say, because it means you haven't thought through the situation thoroughly.

But an entrepreneur who is asking for other people's money should not be asking for what she *wants* to live on, neither her eventual salary goal nor even an amount equal to her current lifestyle demands. An entrepreneur has to ask for what she *needs* to live—and that means preparing for sacrifices.

As an investor, I want a person who is going to sacrifice to get me a return on my investment. Consider an investment pitch that opens like this: "I want you to give me five hundred thousand dollars for a year to fund my business and I'm going to take half of that to live on." No potential investor would be willing to commit to such a plan. I know I would turn it down because in a plan like that, not enough of my money is put to use. What is the incentive for the business owner to work harder if he's already living comfortably?

Now if the entrepreneur were to say, "My bare requirement to live on and to pay for my children's school, my mortgage, and all my bills is seventy-five thousand dollars a year. I need to earn that and I need to earn more than that to be comfortable and have security," then I would be more likely to listen. We could work out a plan where I could tell her, "Maybe there's a way that I'll give you seventy thousand dollars if you hit your targets and another seventy thousand if you exceed your targets."

Too often I meet entrepreneurs who are there to negotiate, and they misread my words when I say, "When you are looking for other people's money, tell people what you *need* versus what you *want*." You should never say "Here's what I want" to an investor unless you're in a position of strength, that is, you have a business that's strong, profitable, growing, and in demand.

I know what it takes to get a business on its feet—and I know that you have to stay hungry for the next sale in order to pour the right kind of energy into your development in the early stages. If you're not uncomfortable, you're not going to be working so hard to create a superior product and pursue clientele.

Take a look at your estimated start-up cost, then divide that number in half. Could you make it work on that amount? Divide it in half again. How about now? Those are the numbers you need to be considering when you anticipate your standard of living. When the available resources are greatly reduced so that you're in survival mode rather than surplus mode, it's amazing how quickly items that seemed to be necessary suddenly become less so. Your essentials shift when your priorities do.

Repeat this same halving of capital with your estimated monthly budget needs. Could you make the business survive—could you survive—on an amount half or even a quarter of what you initially projected? If you find yourself facing that reality, what will you be willing to sacrifice in terms of your business plan and your personal life in order to keep the company afloat? The answer to that question should be "whatever it takes, up to everything I have." Make sure that you account for every necessary expense as you determine the amount of your capital dedicated to self-preservation. This will become that starting point for your business plan.

There is one more step of sacrifice that will be required, and that is your time.

I often jokingly explain entrepreneurship like this: you get to set your own hours—you pick the seventeen hours of the day that are best for you, any seven days of the week. Of course, as exhausting as the hours can be, if you're doing what you love, it doesn't drain you in the way that the previously described Death Cycle does.

Once your company is on firm footing, you'll have far more flexibility and far more freedom, but that doesn't happen overnight. It certainly doesn't happen within the first couple of months either, or even the first few years. Remember that your goals lie further down the road at the five- or ten-year mark. That means you need to be willing to give up your free time now for the sake of having much more of it in the future. Without the sacrifice of personal time, your business will not have sufficient muscle and drive behind it to launch successfully and build momentum.

What it all comes down to in the end is the same refrain that is laced throughout this book: there is no secret by which you can bypass the hard work, sacrifice, headaches, and sweat equity required to establish and grow a business. The advice in this chapter is not optional for an aspiring entrepreneur. It is essential. If you are not willing to make sacrifices, you will not succeed with your business—plain and simple.

# 12

## MILLION-DOLLAR MISTAKES

Before we get into the next few chapters on the technical aspects of getting your business started, I want to talk about some of the harder lessons I learned—my million-dollar mistakes, as I like to call them. I hear people talk about their successes all the time, but not much about their failures. My purpose in writing this book is so you can understand not only who I am and the mind-set that got me here, but also the mistakes I've made in life and business. You'll probably have a good laugh in this chapter. My hope is that you won't make the same million-dollar mistakes I did; but you probably will.

Here are my favorites:

### 1. DON'T MAKE WILDLY OPTIMISTIC SALES FORECASTS.

In 1999, when I was building my business plan for SkyPipeline, we were in the midst of the dot-com boom. The economy was doing great, there were billionaires left and right, IPOs every day, and I had a huge desire to create a multibillion-dollar company out of nothing. I thought the only way I'd be able to secure funding was to make monumental projections.

The funny thing about Excel spreadsheets is that you can build a very successful business in them that has no connection to reality. It was so exciting to see these huge numbers pop up on my spreadsheet that I rationalized the results. In reality, I had no idea how to get my business to such levels, but I knew how to get Excel to get me there, and "there" looked like a lot of fun.

When I went out in search of investors with these numbers, I'd be asked questions I had no idea how to answer, I'd be criticized, and I'd be laughed at. Instead of building the business model on an accurate prediction, I built it on the absolute best-case scenario. And if any of my businesses had actually lived up to these Excel-built expectations, it would have been only because of luck, not because of actual skill or ability.

In the SkyPipeline deal, one of the reasons why I didn't make so much money as I should have was because my forecasts were always off and way too high; the real numbers couldn't match the expectations I had set for my investors.

After a meeting one day, a board member pulled me aside and said, "You had a great month. Sales were up by 20 percent, but you predicted 30 percent. If you'd predicted accurately, you would have gotten high fives all around, but instead you missed your numbers by a third."

After you do that enough times and are humbled by a board that *lives* to humble young entrepreneurs, you learn to forecast your numbers accurately.

Same goes for when Blyth was about to buy ViSalus. At the time, our market in Jamaica was growing rapidly. When asked my opinion on the matter, I said that by the same time next year our sales would be a million dollars a month. I remember Bob Goergen stopping the meeting and saying, "A million, huh? OK, we'll check back in on that number."

Needless to say, at the time of writing this, our Jamaica market does

1 percent of a million dollars a month. And Bob Goergen did check back. I learned my lesson more than once.

It pays greatly to be accurate in your projections.

## 2. DON'T HIRE PEOPLE WHO LIKE YOUR IDEAS *ALL THE TIME*.

When you're just starting out as an entrepreneur, you're selling everyone. First you're selling yourself on the idea, then your investors, your spouse, your mom . . . basically anyone who will buy into what you're doing. And most people don't buy into your crazy idea for revolutionizing the dog food industry.

Occasionally someone will walk into your office looking for a job, and he'll buy everything you're selling. He'll love your ideas. Every time you open your mouth, he'll say, "Yes, sir!" and "Oh, that's amazing!"

You're thinking, *Finally, someone who gets me! He understands my vision!*

And because you're so used to rejection, the flattery goes right to your head, and you hire that person on the spot.

Of course I don't have to tell you how this story turns out: if you hire dumb people, you get a dumb company. Now I look for employees with a high three-digit intelligence. They need to question the things I tell them; think deeply on topics, critically; and be able to beat me in Connect Four.

## 3. DON'T FOCUS TOO MUCH ON THE COMPETITION.

This is a story about how I spent a million dollars trying to get payback from a competitor, and paid dearly.

As you've probably figured out by now, I'm an extremely competitive person. It's really gotten the best of me more than once. When we first started ViSalus and got some momentum going, I started recruiting top people to help us build the business. Well, one of our direct competitors got wind of it, and started dismantling my leadership team by luring away our leaders. (The competitor bribed them with cash and other incentives.)

I had no idea what I was up against, but it was a well-funded army whose sole objective was to take us down. They knocked us on our asses, and sent us down from $1.2 million a month to $300,000 a month. After that I had such great difficulty turning our company around that it was almost as bad as the 2008 recession. Had I not gone through it, however, I never would have made it through the recession.

It was like being back in my juvenile delinquent days when a rival gang figured out where my homeys and I lived. They would keep attacking until we either left the neighborhood or got them back. Well, ViSalus successfully fought off the competition, but in one fell swoop that competition took nearly a million dollars a month in sales with them. They killed a lot of my family.

I swore vengeance.

Fast-forward to 2008, when I'd just sold ViSalus and the economy had started to falter. The very company that had attacked me was suddenly faced with absolute collapse. I remembered so vividly what its people had done to me—the sleepless nights, the loss of employees, the lack of confidence from my shareholders—and because of those memories I let my vindictive side get the best of me. While my competitors scrambled to save their company, it was payback time for me. I started dismantling their leadership team. Not to steal sales but solely for the pleasure of watching them fall. And they did.

In return I got all their disloyal, unsuccessful leaders, spent almost all my company's capital on the effort, and nearly lost ViSalus as a result. In retrospect, that company would have failed with or without my assistance, and if I'd been smart, I'd have put that same money into restructuring our business model to adapt to the new economy earlier. And in the end they would have failed even without my help.

## 4. DON'T WASTE TIME CARING WHAT OTHERS THINK AND WORRYING TOO MUCH ABOUT MISTAKES, EVEN MILLION-DOLLAR ONES.

I used to care too much about whether people liked me or not. For example, if I was off on my numbers—as I often was, thanks to my wildly overoptimistic sales forecasts—I would start talking in circles until I sounded like an idiot. Now no matter how bad it sounds, I say what's on my mind and focus on the solutions, not the problems and my excuses for them. In these situations always remember these five words and twelve letters: it is what it is.

Also, I used to worry about the mistakes I'd made and how close they came to knocking me out of the game. Some people might say, Who cares when you've got nothing to lose? The problem is that when you're a survivor, you actually care a lot about failure. You want to win so badly that you'll rationalize anything just to keep an idea alive.

But in business you have to let the mistakes become part of the process, learn from them, and then move on as quickly as possible. My best victories were rooted in my greatest mistakes.

For instance, at ViSalus, when we launched our weight-loss products, we did it all wrong. We added them as a separate product line to two already successful product lines, thereby giving our customers three lines to choose from. It didn't work. We had to learn from the mistake and relaunch the entire company around the concept of a ninety-day weight-loss challenge. Now our weight-loss line is our growth engine.

If we'd sat around getting mad at ourselves, we never would have relaunched the line correctly. We took a big mistake and learned from it, and then turned it into an absolute success.

As an entrepreneur building a multimillion-dollar business, your failures are going to be your greatest assets, provided you have a philosophy that addresses mistakes, strives to understand them, learns the key elements in them, and turns them into successes.

## 5. DON'T DO YOUR BUSINESS WHERE YOU DO BUSINESS.

After SkyPipeline was sold, I started another business. During the merger of Nexweb and SkyPipeline, one of the guys we'd hired to train our salespeople approached me about an idea for a company that would empower and educate high school kids. Having been an at-risk high school dropout myself, I really got into the idea.

Richard wanted us to start speaking at various high schools and get their parents to buy books, CDs, and so on, to help their children. I jumped right in and went back and spoke at my old high school, and at about six others from LA to Chicago. I started getting passionate about the project. So as I exited SkyPipeline and invested in the new company, called Enspire, we created some simple, free software, and aimed to offer some online goal-setting tools. This was 2003 before social networking had really taken off. Our original idea was to start a social network around people's inspirational and motivational goals and connect them based on other mutual goals.

I dove right in and started hiring people. We had about ten full-time employees in a tight-knit start-up environment, everyone working together in the same room and sitting around a big conference table making phone calls, writing content, booking appointments, and pitching our business to anyone who would listen.

I could tell that one of the women we'd hired had a crush on me. I was recently single at the time, but I decided not to act on it. It's not good business for CEOs to be sleeping with an employee and I could sense it would be trouble.

But I was young. And she was young. I was single. She was single. And one night after a bunch of us had been drinking and partying at an employee's birthday party, this girl offered me a ride home. I don't believe in drinking and driving and she was sober that night, so I jumped into her car and . . .

. . . early the next morning, I was awakened by a phone call from my business partner Richard, and I'm lying in bed next to our employee. Embarrassed, I lied. "Oh, I'm at my house . . ."

I knew I'd made a big mistake, and I swore never to make it again. She was hoping that we'd continue having a relationship. I prayed that she would have the maturity to deal with our actions. We were on completely different pages. I talked to her and explained that as adults, our actions should not impact our working relationship. I told her that I respected her talent or wouldn't have hired her otherwise; what happened was private.

Fast-forward a few weeks. I'd been weighing my actions around the office carefully, so as not to treat anyone more favorably than the others. I was hoping that years down the road, both she and I would look back and be comfortable knowing we'd made a mature decision. Richard called me into the office, and as I walked in, he was standing there staring at me, and the girl was standing in the corner sobbing. "She told me everything," he said. "You've been lying to me. You've been trying to cover this up. You betrayed her, treating her as if she doesn't exist around the office because you're trying to overcompensate. What is she—a notch on your belt?"

I remember saying, "Are you kidding me? We're adults here!"

He absolutely tore into me, and used the moral high ground as his pulpit. I realized that what he was really attempting to do was use this scandal as an opportunity to take control of the company.

I was the funding behind the project and I told him that if he kept it up, it was going to tear apart the company. I went home absolutely overwhelmed. In the meantime, my partner proceeded to call an all-hands meeting, attempting to turn everyone against me. Ten jobs were now on the line, and some of them were my friends and past employees. When the meeting was over, I was informed that they'd decided as a group that I was to come back in a sales role, and (surprise, surprise) Richard would take over the job as CEO.

I was so embarrassed, and humiliation is one of my biggest red buttons. I was furious. I'd quit my job, I had invested a lot of my money, and there was no way my ego would let me come back to work in a sales position when I'd funded the entire business.

They knew there were just enough funds in their bank account (provided by yours truly) to keep going without me. So I left, and Richard agreed to pay me back at least the initial $30,000 I had dropped into the deal.

Turns out Richard was no CEO, and he soon had to close the company. Everyone got walking papers.

It was an absolutely failed venture. When I got the call saying the business was closed, I sent one of my friends to get the computers. I had the ten work stations set up in my loft on the fourteenth floor of the Marina City Club in Marina del Rey (computers were even on my balcony) and started hiring new employees, then proceeded to start a new company called PathConnect out of my living room.

Because of the things I learned while failing at Enspire, when we later merged PathConnect and Solution X, I turned this million-dollar mistake I'd made into a multimillion-dollar windfall.

The moral here is do not fraternize with your employees, and choose your partners wisely. Sometimes people agree to things on paper that they don't understand in reality. And in my opinion, a true partner would have handled this situation much differently. A true partner would have confronted me privately and said, "You screwed up. You lied. We need to talk about this. This is never going to happen again." I would have accepted that. Instead, my partner chose to let his ego kill a lot of jobs, and I vowed never to make the same mistake if I were put in his situation in the future.

This is an extremely tough lesson to learn, however, I know being a hopeless romantic, it's easy to convince yourself that you can be the next Bill and Melinda Gates, who meet at work, fall in love, and are able to build their passion with passion. Unfortunately, the probability of a successful relationship is extremely low, so the likelihood of that happening is far from reality. It's more likely instead of becoming the Gates, you become the McCourt family, a husband and wife who ran their business together and when they divorced they went through a nasty court battle, ultimately both of them publicly disgraced, and forced major league baseball to take over the Dodgers.

In order for you to get this profound lesson deep into your psychology I'm going to use a technique that is uncommon in business education. In fact, I had to do a deep recall into some of the more obscure learning strategies that I have applied in order to firmly anchor lessons into my subconscious mind. This technique requires a chalkboard and chalk—have you guessed it? Write the following words:

Don't do your business where you do business. Don't do your business where you . . .

Trust me, though, you want to learn this lesson without having to go through it yourself.

Thou shalt not "do your business" where you do business.

## 6. DON'T ALLOW SALES EMPLOYEES TO SELL YOU.

Salespeople should not have time to sell their CEOs or any executive other than those of a prospective customer. This is only acceptable during review time, or while handing in a material account. Then you should listen to the pitch. If a member of your team comes to you with poor results but a great sales pitch—fire him. He's spending his time selling you when he's supposed to be *selling*. A good salesperson doesn't have that kind of time.

Which leads me to . . .

## 7. . . . NOT FIRING FAST ENOUGH.

You'll never regret firing someone unless, of course, you let it drag on and they comes back to haunt you by saying they felt misled or wronged. Pull the trigger fast. I've settled enough lawsuits over this one to feed a family of five for ten years.

## 8. DON'T GET CAUGHT UP IN YOUR COMPANY.

A company isn't just an entity; it's a collection of people. Measure the collective passion of your team and the collective intelligence, and you have a company that's either worth something or it's not. Don't get caught up in your logo or the mission statement on the wall. Get caught up in the people who are within those walls.

## 9. DON'T UNDERFORECAST CASH NEEDS.

Just as bad, if not worse, than overly optimistic sales predictions, under-forecasts can also cost you millions. When you have several people and their families depending on you for their paychecks, and you're out of money . . . now that's a nothing-to-lose situation. (If you have a good company, I'll be happy to lend you the money to meet your underfore-casted cash flow—at a very, very expensive cost.) I've taken these types of loans and, believe me, they've cost me clearly.

## 10. DON'T TRY TO DO TOO MUCH ALL AT ONCE.

When I started PathConnect, I was trying to run two businesses at the same time. I thought, *This is great. I'll be just like Steve Jobs with Apple and Pixar.* Yeah, the difference between Steve Jobs and me is that he'd worked with the same high-quality teams for years, and had many more zeroes in his bank account along with significant experience from his days at Apple. I'd had less experience at being an entrepreneur, and not enough money to hire the quality teams I'd need to run the businesses, or, quite honestly, the aptitude to run the companies simultaneously. Lesson learned.

All too often I hear guys say, "I have eight companies!" Unless you're Warren Buffett, do not own eight companies. What's the good in having six businesses that make less than $100,000 a year when you could own just one that makes $1.6 million a year? As the old saying goes: A bird in the hand is worth more than two in the bush.

## 11. NEVER WRITE SOMETHING YOU WOULDN'T WANT TO COME BACK TO YOU.

Just after I sold SkyPipeline, I got kind of lazy. I knew I was going to make a lot of money, I was young, and I was already looking forward to the playboy lifestyle I would soon be leading.

One day I showed up at the office late and seven days unshaved. It was Halloween, and all I had on my mind was what I was going to do that evening. I'd planned to take my crew to the Playboy Mansion. We had limos lined up, girls invited, and we were going to have the time of our lives.

Because I had nothing to do, and because I hated the people I was working for, I decided to sit down and craft an e-mail to "my boys" about the evening's festivities. I went into great detail about the night's plans. I told them where we'd be going, what they needed to avoid, and even . . . what to bring to "protect" themselves.

I ended the e-mail by telling them that they had no need to worry about anything except what they'd be wearing. Everything else, including the limos, bottle service and after party, would be paid for from the sale of my company. I, personally, would be wearing a cloak and mask, just like Tom Cruise in *Eyes Wide Shut*. And as you can tell, I like to write, so I went on to describe in every detail how we would conquer our objectives that Halloween evening.

I went into Outlook, clicked on the address group called "the boys," and pressed send.

Next I sat at my desk, eagerly waiting for the first response from the seven or eight true friends on the list who, I supposed, were dying laughing. The first e-mail came in titled "Re: Festivities," but it was from one of my investors, Fred Warren. It said, "Ryan, I'm going to wear a pink tutu to the event and I can't wait to see you!"

I was totally puzzled. How the hell did our chairman, Fred Warren, get into my e-mails? Was he spying on the server? I went back to Outlook and realized, to my absolute horror, that I hadn't sent it to "the boys" after all—I'd sent it to "the bod," our board of directors.

As you know, my board was composed of billionaires, titans of industry, world-renowned venture capitalists and businessmen, men whom I had worked very hard to earn respect from.

One after the other, they started replying "to all," each letting me know what they would be wearing and whether they could make it. Scot Jarvis said he planned to fly in for the event. Others said they weren't going to make it, but were really disappointed. It was an absolute disgrace.

I broke into a red sweat. In a panic, I frantically hit the recall button (a feature that doesn't do anything except notify the person you sent the e-mail to that you regretted sending it). I freaked out for hours. I reread the e-mail again and again, wondering how they'd interpreted it. What had I done? Was this the end of me? Meanwhile, the board continued to bask in my embarrassment.

All because I'd hit "the bod" instead of "the boys."

I will never again put something in writing that I wouldn't want to come back to me. And furthermore, I've made it a personal policy never to use the auto-fill function of Outlook again when sending e-mails. I've seen this feature bite a few other people in the ass.

## 12. DON'T DATE THE WRONG WOMEN.

Or the wrong men. This should be self-explanatory.

## 13. DON'T INVEST IN UNCOACHABLE ENTREPRENEURS.

For example, the Make the Difference Network (MTDN) had a failed business model, and the two entrepreneurs behind it cost me and several others more than a million in cash because of it. Here's an e-mail between the founders and me.

From: Ryan Blair

Sent: Tuesday, March 04, 2008 11:31 AM

To: ███████

Subject: Today's call

███, In preparation for today's call to discuss your need for additional financing, I thought I would give you my perspective and some things to think about prior to.

I am still a believer in what MTDN could be to the world, however I am not confident in where we are as partners as of today. I know from talks with the internal PathConnect team that you continue to fault us for your inability to drive revenue and execute on your business. And we find ourselves investing a disproportionate amount of time and effort into the project helping to fill operational gaps and going beyond the call of duty at times, doing what we can to help move the business forward, despite it all. As you know I am sensitive to your perspective on our work as it impacts the morale of our team and at present the people here working on MTDN are starting to express negative sentiment . . . especially in consideration of the following:

To date, we've spent $394,000, specifically on the MTDN site development. We've loaned the company $30,000, purchased $55,000 worth of sponsorships and services, in addition Chris and John Tolmie have loaned $75,000 . . . to bridge the company while it seeks financing. This brings our group's total spend to $504,000. As a start-up ourselves, this capital is very significant as it represents our time, money and opportunity to become a profitable business.

I believe we are at a critical decision point in both of our
businesses and our continued relationship. As I see it, we only
have 3 options:

1. You take the independent route, accept the ███████
investment (which is a fair deal from our BOD's perspective), and
we define our final deliverables, and continued maintenance
requirements for our 25% equity position.

2. You integrate completely into the PathConnect group, we take
a controlling interest and double down our efforts while working
toward being profitable together.

3. We decide that our differences are insurmountable, and we
restructure the relationship, whereby we own less equity and
have limited further obligations toward the building of the MTDN
product.

In my humble opinion, there is no option where our group (or
myself personally for that matter) continues to provide bridge
financing. In light of the aforementioned

I hope we can find a solution!

Sincerely,

Ryan J. Blair

Chairman

ViSalus/PathConnect

He decided to raise money from others. I wanted to run with MTDN,
but despite my efforts, these entrepreneurs absolutely refused to listen to
me, or all the other smart businesspeople I surrounded them with, including Jay Fulcher, CEO of Agile (Oracle bought Agile for $500 mil-
lion); Todd Goergen; and a host of other prominent businessmen and
investors. I got Paul Allen, cofounder of Microsoft, to show up at my

house to meet the spokesperson, Jessica Biel, to talk about the project. We even hosted the Clinton Global Initiative and got former president Bill Clinton to promote us. We sent out Jessica Biel to talk the company up and pulled enough strings to get Chris Cuomo to endorse the project on *Good Morning America*.

But a great project doesn't mean a good business. To use Fred Warren's expression, "I broke my pick on them." I spent all my energy trying to persuade the founders to change their business model.

They were so caught up in their own ideas that they decided to go their own way. And a few short weeks prior to this writing, I went to their Web site and saw that they're officially out of business. I hate being right when I'm predicting that I'll lose money.

I hope they'll learn from their mistakes. I learned a lot, and MTDN actually led to the creation of the Body By Vi Community Challenge, from which we've raised enough funds for more than five hundred thousand meals for at-risk kids. This is one of the cornerstones of the ViSalus community. We utilized the valuable insights we gained from our work on MTDN to launch our cause marketing campaign and to make cause marketing a core of our work in the local communities we participate in.

So there you have them, my million-dollar mistakes. The irony here is that I never imagined that I would have enough money to make million-dollar mistakes. In truth, I've probably wasted more in mistakes and the resulting lost opportunities than I've made in income. But I've been able to do very well for myself despite my setbacks, so I guess the moral of this chapter is that you should try not to do what I did. If you have to, you can make as many of your own million-dollar mistakes as you like (as long as you can afford them), then eventually apply what you've learned, and win.

In the following chapters I will get into the nuts and bolts of starting your business. Without technical understanding, you don't have anything, so I urge you, when you are ready, to read this material. Starting your own business is not easy, and nothing is guaranteed, but if you are smart, you will have the right strategies and business expertise to increase your odds of success.

# 13

## I HATE BUSINESS PLANS

---

Most business plans aren't worth the paper they're written on.

And most entrepreneurs write business plans that are a bunch of fluff about how "through strategic partnerships" we will "maximize efficiencies" and "combine market place opportunities." Is there any value in the aforementioned statement? None at all. Most plans that are sent to me are closed within a few seconds of opening them. The best business plan is one built from a business that is already up and running and forecasts the business's potential growth.

A business plan can be built on the back of a napkin because the plan part is simple. But there is a lot of prep work required before you can write on the back of a napkin a plan that actually works. You first need to do a lot of soul-searching, have serious discussions with your family, and shift to entrepreneurial thinking. And if you've done all that—save that napkin. It might be worth something someday. Like the one the guys at Yahoo have hanging on their wall.

A business plan is simple. Take the plan you've probably been composing in your head and have written on various scratch pads for a long time, and put it in an executive summary that is no more than three pages long. Make it clear and base it on reality or your best guess of the potential of the business. This will be the platform from which you reach out to potential investors and clients. That's it. Three pages of clear, concise business objectives, expected results, and the strategy to get there. Easier said than done, right?

The focus of this chapter is not to help you determine whether you should become an LLC or a C Corporation or to instruct you in how to manage the patent process. There are great online resources, such as the U.S. Small Business Adminstration's Web site (www.sba.gov), to help walk you through those parts of the process of formulating your business plan.

Instead, I want to focus on the mind-set you will need as you enter into this phase of your business: what to consider, what to keep in the back of your mind, and what to watch for as you bring your business to life from page to pavement.

Before you begin creating spreadsheets and crunching numbers, though, I suggest that you begin your business plan by writing a personal purpose statement in which you outline the philosophies and vision that you want for you and the company you are creating. Post this where you can see it while you're working on your budgets and potential client lists. Keep a copy in your wallet so you have it with you when you make spending decisions. A tangible, visible reminder of your goals and ideals will help keep your focus and your mind in the right place as you create the plan your business will follow.

In 2003, I sat down to create a purpose statement for my own self-goals, and I created the following document:

> My purpose in life is to inspire the minds and actions of others in harmony with myself and with the minds of the people by whom I am inspired. I will lead others to their own personal greatness. I will mobilize an unstoppable army of like-minded individuals to achieve extraordinary results. I will help those in need and give the gift of an independent life to thousands of willing minds. I will give independence from abuse and self-destruction, independence from

confusion, and independence from economic burdens. I will identify my unsuccessful beliefs and remove all beliefs that do not suit my purpose in life.

In this pursuit, I will learn to identify GREATNESS in others with extreme accuracy, and I will hold myself accountable for all of my actions. I will operate with integrity, and I will seek feedback from others with an open mind for self-improvement.

I will focus only on items I am deeply passionate about, items at which I can be the best in the world.

I will set my mark as an individual who overcame great obstacles to achieve extraordinary success. I will help, both directly and indirectly, millions of people to do the same.

I will measure my influence by the network of people I can draw upon for inspiration and economic creation.

As you can see from my personal purpose statement, it is nothing especially profound. It doesn't have to be. It just needs to be an honest declaration of the principles by which you intend to operate and the goals that you hope to achieve through your efforts. I have continued to revise, rewrite, and rework this original purpose statement as my situation has changed, but the core ideals and the vision remain the same. The irony is that in December 2003, I had no idea what I was going to do. Looking at my purpose statement now, I can tell you that I am on the path toward achieving the results I dreamed of through the companies I am a part of. With clarity of purpose as an individual, you will have clarity in your business; after all, you are your business.

I urge you to take the time to complete this step before moving on to the more technical parts of your business plan. The perspective and direction a purpose statement can give you will be invaluable for the days when you want to give up, when you're questioning why you ever jumped into the world of entrepreneurship in the first place.

You are now ready to start the actual plans for the business itself. One of the most important of these, and one of the earliest ones to focus on, is your company's name. I cannot emphasize enough how important it is to come up with the right name. Enlist family members and friends to help, bounce ideas off one another, and take note of which ones get positive reactions and which ones get confused looks.

## YOUR BUSINESS NAME, NOT YOUR PORN NAME

When I decided to write this book, I had no idea what to title it. In an interview I did on CNBC's *The Big Idea* with Donny Deutsch, Donny asked me, "How did you figure this out? Where did this drive come from?"

I answered, "I lost everything and found myself in a position where I had nothing to lose."

I immediately searched to see if NothingToLose.com was available and, as you can imagine, it wasn't. That didn't stop me. I looked up who its owner was, and that led to a company called DomainMarket.com, which had it for sale on their site for $35,000. I contacted them, and because they were inspired by the project, they agreed to sell me the URL for a reduced amount. It's still the most expensive domain name I've ever bought, but it was worth it to me to have that connection to my book. I tell you this to stress that your business name is extremely important, and the brand equity it creates may one day be your most valuable asset.

If you have a good name, it will stick with people, which does as much to give you brand recognition as does a catchy jingle or slick logo.

Take, for example, Airborne. It's got a great story and a compelling hook, but it also has an extremely smart name. The maker chose a word that has meaning because many cold viruses are spread through the air. We human beings hate the thought of somebody sneezing in our proximity; we'll hold our breath or try to breathe in the other direction—especially in an enclosed area like an airplane or a classroom. So the product name plays to the common fear, but it gives it a positive spin—it's a way to fight back against the common airborne illnesses we all dread. It's catchy and simple and easy to remember.

The selection of your name should be something that helps tell your story so it sparks continued interest in your product. Think about Google. It wasn't just selected because it's a funny-sounding word; it is the mathematical term for an unimaginably large number—one with one hundred zeros after it. That's a smart name. It sounds unique, so it sticks with you, but it also has a relevant meaning and clues you in to the product and the company itself.

Some people want to have their names in their titles, such as Thompson & Sons Furniture Company. That is a fine option, too, if you are creating something you want to be your legacy as a family owned and operated company.

I know that some people are a little leery of having a name that reveals the company to be a family-based business because they fear the perception of being a small-time operation. I believe, however, that we are in the midst of a major trend that is orienting toward family-run companies. Most of us would rather support a locally owned business than a global corporation—we want to keep our money in the area and give our business to the people who have stuck their necks out and worked hard to establish a reputation in our community. I think a lot of this is tied to Americans' natural tendency to side with the underdog, but I think it also has to do with some of the major news stories over the past number of years concerning companies like Enron and various business schemes. There isn't necessarily safety in size anymore. Corporate greed disgusts us, and as our confidence is shaken by stories of unethical and hugely harmful practices, I believe that the value of face-to-face service and accountability will continue to grow in the minds of consumers.

Make a list of all of the adjectives you would like people to associate with your business, and then narrow it down to your top three or four. Using those words as your reference point, try to come up with names that match that image. You may need to dedicate a lot of time to finding just the right name that fits you and fits your business because this will be the backbone of your brand.

This search for a name can be one of the most satisfying steps in the entire process, because once your company has one, not only will you be able to use that title on all of the legal paperwork, you'll also be able to think of your business in a solid, this-is-really-going-to-happen kind of way. Much like selecting a name for an unborn baby, settling on a name for your business can make the reality seem more real. It can help you wrap your brain around the excitement and the size of the undertaking you're about to face.

If all else fails, you can combine the name of the street you grew up on with your middle name, and then you'll have a business porn name. Mine would be Bella Vista Jerry. Sounds like a Mexican ice-cream truck. Maybe my future is calling.

## GAME THEORY

All jokes aside, as you pore over names and sort through options in the back of your mind, you should also start on the practical side of the business plan by compiling a comprehensive list of funding sources. Look back at what you listed during the phase of evaluating your assets to begin figuring out how to tailor your plan to land investors' interest. You need to figure out what is going to make your business plan stand out from the hundreds of other business plans that get pitched to investors each day. What is your niche in the market? What need are you filling that no one else is? What can you do better than anyone else?

A good way to think about finding your business's unique place in the market is to look at what researchers call game theory. If two people are locked in a struggle to earn a prize, what will each one do to get ahead?

The most common hypothetical scenario is that of two people who are tied together at the ankles and teetering at the edge of a cliff. The first one to back down loses. If one person starts jumping around or kicking his legs over the edge, the other person is likely to give up sooner—even if it means forfeiting the prize—because he becomes too nervous. The person who did the jumping around held what is referred to as the "dominant strategy." That is, he took some risks and did something unusual to force his opponent to surrender.

In many ways, the business world is very similar. Most businesses are content to stay right at the edge of the cliff, barely breathing and praying the wind doesn't pick up to send them hurtling off the edge. In other words, they are passively trying to win. If you are willing to enter the contest with a dominant strategy, the difference of your approach to theirs is what will ultimately make you successful. Trying something that hasn't been done can be risky, but it can also distinguish you in a way that leads to greater gains.

That dominant strategy is what you should be hammering out as you formulate your business plan. The unique offerings or unusual approach you take when meeting a need or solving a problem should be your focus. That should be the reason you are starting this entire venture. No one is interested in another company that does the same thing as everyone else—a "me too" company.

When I was first launching SkyPipeline, it was a challenge to establish our place in the market. It was Southern California, and the tech bubble was still going strong, so there were many growing broadband service providers competing for the same clientele. I started my company without a fully developed business plan—the numbers were all there, but I hadn't realized the importance of thinking about emphasizing our differentiation from every other company out there.

Finally, in one investment pitch, the venture capitalist asked me why he should choose my company to invest in over any of the dozens of other plans on his desk. I took a gamble: I picked up the phone and asked him to call our company's number. I promised him that as a broadband wireless company, we would always have someone there to answer the phones promptly, and at a call center that was not located halfway around the world. It was a cold call. My staff had no idea I would be phoning the center, and I held my breath and hoped that my employees would represent our company well. Sure enough, the phone rang, a live person answered, my investor was impressed, and we got the capital to keep our business growing. Our greatest differentiation was in our customer service, and that's exactly what we focused on. And no big phone company could compete with that.

I had been wasting time pitching other services and features ahead of our guaranteed quick-response policy. What I should have been concentrating on was the fact that we had mastered all of the usual frustrations of trying to get decent tech support and provided a faster and more reliable service than our competitors did.

Now THAT WE'RE done talking about game theory, let's talk about the hard numbers and budgeting proposals, which are probably what most people think of when they imagine drawing up a business plan.

You will need to account for all start-up costs, including any licensing fees, certifications, equipment purchases, employee salaries, and retail or office space required to open the doors to your business. I cannot offer specific advice as to the needs or vision of each individual company. I will urge you, however, to do your research through books, magazines, and online sources, and by interviewing other entrepreneurs to make sure you have as full and complete a picture as possible for the needs of your business. And as I mentioned, you should have a contingency plan in place in case you have to operate on far less than your projected amount.

The start-up costs will vary a great deal from person to person and business to business, just as day-to-day operational costs will. For example, if you are planning to open a photography business, you may decide to be only an on-location photographer at first, shooting weddings and family portraits on the beach or in local public gardens. If you wish to establish a studio side of the operation to go along with your event shooting, then you need to make room for the required costs in your plan. It may be wise to establish phases for your business to help defray the start-up costs, like starting without a storefront while you establish a clientele, but with plans to open one in six months or a year.

Something I learned when writing my very first business plan is that there are really two different plans you need to come up with. You need to have an operations plan as well as a plan to raise money. The operations plan will be centered on your specific business model—how you plan to operate and structure your company. The fund-raising presentation should focus more on the industry, the growth projections, the competition, and your position within the marketplace. It should also profile similar companies that have been successful and that have successfully exited. You need to include some of this information in your operations plan, but it is central to your fund-raising plan because it demonstrates an in-depth, working knowledge of the realm you're seeking to enter.

I start with my operational plan and develop that first before moving on to the financial plan. The creation of your operational plan needs to be a bottom-up procedure. Don't start with a number in mind; start from zero and then add expenses and capital requirements, broken down to their most basic components. You should ask yourself, "What do I absolutely have to have to operate this business, and what will that cost me each month?"

To create a hypothetical situation, look at it this way: How many units do I need to sell per month in order to cover my expenses? If the answer is one hundred, then determine how many units the average salesperson can sell. If the answer is ten, then you know you will need at least ten salespeople—or you need to have marketing that will drive some portion of those sales, say 50 percent, in which case you know you need five people and X dollars in marketing to generate the orders. But for those five or ten employees, you need to figure out their true expense. How much does it cost to recruit them? What will you pay them? How much of their pay will be generated through commissions? Will you be providing them with a cell phone or a laptop? How will you fund their sales calls? But don't just write down a number and move on. You need to consider carefully every minuscule part of the potential cost: Will you pay your employees' mileage if they use their own cars? How will you pay for their travel if they need to fly? Will you pay them a per diem? How much money will you provide for each meal? What about lodging?

You have to remember that every single one of those numbers on the page represents a series of decisions about costs that you need to have considered in order to have a firm grasp on the real price of things.

One of the most important things to remember while planning projected costs and budgets is the determination of what your family is going to live on. As we discussed in the preceding chapters, this number should be conservative, but also realistic. You will need to make sure you factor in the real costs your family will be facing not only for your current bills and financial obligations, but also for future costs you may incur, such as a health insurance policy if you lose coverage when you change jobs. These costs need to be included in your plan, or you will find yourself unable to meet your obligations in the first month, which will put your entire business in jeopardy.

I want to give you a strong word of caution about being overly optimistic. Of course you should believe in your company's potential, but as I've mentioned, it's far too easy to create a million-dollar company on an Excel spreadsheet. On paper, it doesn't seem so far-fetched to count on exponential growth—in the first month you grow 20 percent, then 20 percent again in the second month, and in a matter of just a few months, your entire company has doubled in size. Unfortunately, real growth doesn't work that way. You have to write a realistic plan that considers each transaction and various expenses like marketing support and sales. Your investors will turn on you if you miss your numbers. A mentor and former board member of mine, Gordon Watson, once told me, "Ryan, a CEO has never been fired for missing his numbers, only for missing his forecasts." I took his point seriously, but not seriously enough, as you read in chapter 12, "Million-Dollar Mistakes."

As you reach the completion of your business plan and feel you have your numbers solidly in place, it may be worthwhile to make a small investment in hiring an accountant or a lawyer to look it over and double check that everything looks right. Obviously, she may not be able to speak to the specific circumstances of starting a business in your field, but she can ensure that what you've designated for salaries, taxes, insurance, and any other legally required costs are in line with and appropriate to the size of the company you are establishing.

Also, as elementary as it sounds, you will want to carefully proofread every element of your plan more than once. Read it word for word, and aloud, if you have to. Correct anything that sounds wordy, awkward, or unclear, and definitely check for typos. It's an unfortunate truth, but given the number of business plans investors get each year, they are all looking for a reason to eliminate each one to quickly pare down their "to consider" stack. Typos can come across as careless, and no one wants to invest in a company whose CEO is not detail oriented. Treat your business plan just as you would your own résumé if you were applying for a job with the investor, because, in a way, that's exactly what it is—a résumé for your company. Make sure your first impression is a positive one. If you are going to submit a plan to me, make sure it is concise. If there's one thing that makes me dismiss a plan quickly, it's a plan that is too verbose. These days, a PowerPoint presentation with no more than fifteen slides is all you need for your investor presentation.

And that's why I hate business plans, because the good ones take thousands of hours to create, and then can be summarized on the back of a napkin. And you'll look at the napkin more than the plan. Welcome to the world of entrepreneurship.

# 14

## PROS AND CONS OF
## A HOME-BASED BUSINESS

---

So far, we've discussed a lot of concepts about building businesses that are specific to traditional business, and some that are universal to all business types. In this chapter I want to speak specifically of the principles contained within *Nothing to Lose* that are unique to direct sales and network marketing. I'll be pointing out the areas where traditional business and network marketing align and where they diverge, explaining why home-based business is the solution for a new economy. Finally, so you can get the most out of your chosen path, I'll give you tips and advice based on my seven-year experience in the industry as CEO of ViSalus.

You might have heard of network marketing before. It has names like Ponzi scheme, pyramid scheme, scam, multilevel marketing or MLM, and direct selling. It's known for overly aggressive salesmen, sharks, and snake oil.

I'm here to tell you—it's all true. In many network marketing companies, across the entire industry, you will find all the above, and more.

Having built a network marketing company from the ground up, I can tell you that there are many shortcomings to this vehicle of entrepreneurship. And it's not for everyone. When network marketing is at its worst, it tries, through influence techniques and manipulation, to persuade someone who is consumer minded or employee minded to start a business. And once this has happened, it has created a situation where someone suddenly, overnight, starts spouting an entirely new belief system and talking about how passionate he is about becoming a millionaire.

Think of how ridiculous it would sound if one of your closest friends came to you one day and said, "Hey, I didn't tell you, but I've been secretly working on starting a business. I just opened a restaurant down the street."

"What? Oh my God, are you serious?"

"Yeah, I want all my friends to eat there all the time now. And that includes you."

"Um . . . you're crazy."

"We're having Monday night football specials! And a happy hour! Are you coming?"

"Absolutely not."

That's exactly what happens when someone who isn't prepared, willing, or capable of running any business starts a network marketing business. It shifts his identity immediately. All of a sudden he's preaching principles of success and wealth and completely alienating his friends and family. And in return, these friends and family start forming negative opinions about network marketing and project them onto the person who's recently converted.

Another problem in network marketing is a lopsided ratio of customers to distributors. Let me tell you that during the last six years at ViSalus, we've had to tweak our compensation plan again and again to get it right. It's the most complex system I've ever created, even more complicated than any of the software we had to write for the tech companies I've owned. That's why so many people get it wrong. And that's why so many companies out there are schemes. The sad part is that a lot of them aren't even schemes on purpose.

From my own philosophies in chapter 4: "compensation drives behavior" and if the incentive is in the wrong place, it will produce the wrong behavior.

For example, if people are paid more to recruit new distributors than new customers, they will naturally try to turn everyone into distributors. If they are paid equally, then they will give people a choice—would you like to become a distributor or a customer? If they are paid more to convert people into customers, they will lead with a customer value proposition right from the start.

We learned this firsthand at ViSalus because at first we put too much incentive on recruiting distributors, and as a result all our sales force cared about was converting people into distributors. When the economy fell apart, we had to ask ourselves what we needed to do to meet the needs of our customers. Now if we have a million customers, we have around a hundred thousand distributors, which means that one distributor handles ten customers. And now we're one of the leading companies in the industry.

But so many companies have the ratio wrong, and have millions of distributors and few customers. And those don't work. We figured out that our incentives were creating behaviors in our salespeople that we weren't comfortable with. And that happens all the time, like weeds growing in a garden—it is the nature of a complex business model.

Network marketing was built on the same inauthentic platform that the aforementioned personal growth industry was built on. "Follow me and do as I say," and behind the scenes, they're laughing about all the suckers they've taken in.

Just as I said, there will be a new generation of companies to accommodate a rapidly evolving industry. Network marketing used to exist solely in the privacy of living room parties, and closed-door Amway conventions, and nobody knew exactly how these companies were operating. Now we have the Internet and anyone can get information about any company in existence. It's forcing the industry to change, and ushering in a whole new era.

So in short, absolutely do not join a network marketing company unless you do your due diligence. And you have to *love* the products or service the company provides. Don't let anyone pressure you into starting a business if you don't feel ready, no matter how tempting the sales pitch is. You should know the people you'll be working with, and make sure they have a set of values similar to yours.

But if you do believe that network marketing is for you, then you can start considering yourself an entrepreneur. This might surprise you, but my personal definition of a professional entrepreneur isn't a millionaire. A professional entrepreneur, in my opinion, is anyone who has taken himself off the "job wanted" list. Just like athletes who have started making a full-time income through their chosen sport, they are considered pro. Likewise, the day you start making a full-time income through entrepreneurship, you will be a professional entrepreneur.

If one of your main goals as an entrepreneur is financial independence, then the network marketing route offers some of the quickest low-risk ways to achieve it.

It might not have occurred to you that being self-employed is becoming an entrepreneur. These days we associate entrepreneurship with Facebook and Google, and the dot-com era, when young entrepreneurial upstarts were glorified in popular media. The publicity implied that the route to entrepreneurship was open only to twenty- or thirtysomethings with a high tolerance for risk and an idea for a traditional business venture (one that you start from scratch). We consider the great ones—Ted Turner, Sam Walton, Steve Jobs, and Bill Gates—the only true definitions of a successful entrepreneur. Actually, nothing could be further from the truth. Not only do many entrepreneurs take alternate routes like network marketing, they do it at all ages.

Anyone, at any age, can become self-employed, but traditional business might not be for everyone. For instance, you may have a great idea, but you don't have the start-up capital or the experience in raising funds. You might have the funding, but lack the desire to commit all your time to an entrepreneurial pursuit. Or you may have had a traditional business in the past, and don't want to go through the headache and pain ever again. You may be the type of person who has neither the know-how nor the funding, and are looking at a lot to learn. Network marketing is the perfect opportunity for you to learn the most important functions of any business: sales and marketing. When you master sales and marketing, you are the master of your destiny.

In the old economy (1998–2008), people were attracted to network marketing for its side benefits. The idea of working from home, traveling, making some extra income, and employing the tax advantages appropriate to a home-based business were the primary drivers for the industry.

In the new economy, and for the next decade, people will choose network marketing for its main benefit: the potential financial independence that comes with being a professional entrepreneur. Another reason people are choosing network marketing at a record pace is certainly one of the most attractive qualities about the industry—its flexibility.

Unlike traditional business, you have the option of committing as much or as little time and energy to your network marketing business as you like.

Accordingly, there are three levels of network marketer—beginner, intermediate, and professional.

A beginner is interested in a part-time business where she commits a few hours a week, follows a simple selling system that is prescribed for her by the company she represents, and makes extra income while living a better lifestyle and having fun with the community aspects of network marketing. In some companies your products are free, which saves money, and you get to enjoy all the tax benefits of being an entrepreneur. That means you can write off meetings, your home office, your cell phone bill, educational components like books, classes, travel, and everything else that goes into career development. Low expenses, no overhead, no employees, time freedom, and residual income are all benefits of the industry, but in my opinion they are still overshadowed by the greatest benefit of being a network marketer—the education.

Running a multilevel marketing home-based business is the equivalent of hands-on business school training, with a focus on networking and marketing. In the process you learn personal growth, financial literacy, time management, and all the basics that could also be applied directly to any business you may own or work for in the future.

We've already discussed defining your assets and the low start-up costs for a home-based business, which sometimes can be as low as a few hundred dollars. It's true, with network marketing you don't need a storefront, or investors, or a business plan, or a large capital outlay, but there are other things you'll need, minor investments for your business as a network marketer.

You could start with investing in a smart phone and a good phone plan, as you'll be doing most of your business by phone. You'll need access to a computer to read your reports and manage your business along the way, and if you don't already have a vehicle, it would be a good idea to have a car so you can get around from one client to the next (that's why a lot of network marketing companies, including ViSalus, have car incentive programs). Another recommendation would be to set up Facebook and Twitter accounts, so you can start connecting with all the people you'll be sharing your new venture with.

This leads me to one of the main objections I hear most often—that people are afraid of network marketing because it means they will have to start selling to their friends. If I may be blunt, that's also an "old economy" mind-set. As an entrepreneur, I have always sold my products and services to my friends.

Here's another complaint: "I don't have any friends." Well, that means we have to start from scratch with you, but that's okay. Because these days we can make friends and expand our networking circles through social media, and your friends may be willing to help you. They may even need the product you're offering. It's natural to share something you love; we do it every time we recommend good books (I hope you'll recommend this one) or a movie to our friends.

Let's be honest, if you want to change your financial situation, you're going to have to sell something to someone. Most important, you're going to have to sell yourself to people. Make sure they know that they need YOU and your product and service. On a side note, if a company is worth its salt, it will have a selling system in place that doesn't force you to sell to your friends, but instead provides opportunity to share the products you love with them. Sharing can be done through samples, tastings, or even free trials.

In addition to the minimum requirements I've just outlined, I suggest that people put their assets (see chapter 10) to work. For instance, use their home for parties and networking events as well as office space. A good example would be when I let one of the ViSalus distributors use my home for an Oscar party, where he also used the space and opportunity to share our products with his friends. The way I see it, my house is an asset that I might as well put to work, and there's always an excuse for a party!

Most important, you'll need the ability to follow a simple system. As you progress from one level to the next, you will graduate from following simple systems to implementing them for others to follow. And if you can't learn to follow one, you certainly can't learn to implement one.

And of course, you'll need the right mind-set. Even as a beginner, you are now a business owner. Don't let the low start-up cost fool you into giving up too easily, or not taking the business so seriously as you should. Treat it as if you've invested everything you have into it, and are willing to do whatever it takes to be a successful entrepreneur.

The distinction between a beginning network marketer and an intermediate one includes extra time commitment, the use of a business plan, and, of course, the amount of money you'll be generating per month.

Let's start with the time commitment, which varies depending on the income desired and the relevant experience each person has. Generally, a beginner is making a part-time income, for instance, a thousand dollars a month, which requires a minimum of an hour or two a day. Full time is forty-plus hours a week, and millionaires tend to work eighty- to a hundred-hour weeks on their way there. After they've arrived, so to speak, they can reduce the hours and enjoy the fruits of their labor. On a personal note, I still work eighty-plus hours because I enjoy what I do.

We covered building a business plan in chapter 13, and this is where it becomes relevant. In the beginning stages of network marketing, you won't need a business plan because your team leader or company will provide it for you. In the intermediate stages you will need to start creating a business plan, and at the professional level you will need a more specific business plan.

One of the main differences between owning a traditional business and being a network marketer is that you own your business, but as in a franchise arrangement, you can leverage the parent company's resources, infrastructure, and products. You're not just doing it alone. Most entrepreneurs are owned by their businesses, not the other way around.

As an intermediate, you'll begin adding personal touches to your business. For instance, setting up a name for your team is just as important as naming a restaurant or storefront in traditional business.

Although you won't be hiring employees, the equivalent of "staffing the office" in network marketing is recruiting. You can't hire or fire people or provide benefits, but you can certainly elect whom you want to work with, whom you recruit, and whom you choose to help grow.

Another big difference is that unlike in a traditional business, you have thousands of entrepreneurs, a volunteer army of people whom you work for, not who are working for you. Did you get that? I'll repeat it—you work for them; they don't work for you.

Sounds like a lot of pressure, doesn't it? It's actually one of the best features about being in network marketing because we're all working together, in alignment as entrepreneurs.

It's a working business ecosystem, where like-minded people can learn from one another. In traditional business, the interactions between two business owners are often limited by one being a buyer and one a seller; they can't really work together. But as a traditional business owner in network marketing, you can provide value to the network you are a part of. For instance, Maggie Richardson is a ViSalus distributor who also has a therapeutic massage practice, and she uses her network to spread the word about her services as she builds both businesses.

As I mentioned previously, compensation drives behavior. When network marketing is at its finest, you are compensated for teaching people how to be successful entrepreneurs. It's a compensation system in which teachers make a small percentage of their students' productivity for life. If only our American education system worked the same way. Imagine teachers being rewarded for the productivity of their students!

## IT'S ALL ABOUT RECRUITING

In network marketing, you're not doing it alone. That's why recruiting is one of the most important aspects of your business. Similar to the way UCLA coach John Wooden described the hand-selection process he used when building and cultivating a well-run basketball team, you want to focus on chemistry and finding entrepreneurs within your team who can augment your weaknesses. For instance, if you're not the most detail-oriented person, you'll need to find detail-oriented people for your team. Or if you're great with detail, but more introverted than extroverted, then you'll need someone who's comfortable getting up in front of the room to make presentations. Also, if you don't have the time to commit to your business, there may be others working with you who do.

Which brings me to how much time it takes to become a professional network marketer. I previously referenced Malcolm Gladwell's *Outliers* quote that it takes 10,000 hours to become pro at your chosen industry. And it remains true for network marketing as well as for traditional business. All too often I see network marketing entrepreneurs give up before they log their ten thousand hours.

At the professional level, you'll be traveling the globe, creating marketing campaigns and incentives for your sales team, and making millions. You might have a storefront, offices, and staff, or a really big house that acts as the equivalent of an office or storefront, and essentially be running a big, complex business that spans multiple markets, cultures, and countries.

That's what excited me about this industry. At the pro level, your content is your greatest asset. You can create books and tools, and I've even seen some go so far as to have their own closed-circuit TV shows. You can innovate and create, and build systems and tools to support your team. A professionally run network marketing company is a traditional business, without all the "employee" headaches.

In fact, a lot of people who join network marketing own, or have at one time owned, a traditional business or franchise. I've recruited a number of traditional business owners who see an opportunity to put their assets to work right away in network marketing. They have social capital, relevant education and experience, and they've essentially been creating a perfect business plan their entire careers. These are the ones who advance to the professional level the fastest because they have underutilized assets and relevant experience they can put to work.

But on the opposite side of the equation, there are plenty of people who've never done anything like this, and it's the scariest thing they've ever heard of. Network marketing also works for them, but it usually takes them several years to get to the pro level, and in most cases, the amount of time is determined by how long it takes them to log their ten thousand hours.

As a professional, your goal is to monetize your resources. When you're a millionaire, a lot of people are going to ask you: How do I get what you have? One of the differences is that often in traditional business you can't duplicate and teach someone's road to success. He may have started at the bottom of a company, started from scratch as a delivery boy, or have worked in an industry or economy that has evolved and no longer applies in today's economy. But the path to success in network marketing can be duplicated. You have a built-in vehicle, a curriculum that creates success using work ethic and education.

A lot of what you'll be doing as a professional network marketer is mentoring people. You have to get out and shake hands and spend time with your team members, giving them advice as they grow from level to level. And that's what I find I'm doing the most now after five years in the industry: helping others overcome internal and external obstacles while building their businesses into full-time income to support themselves and their families.

I know that network marketing, as a business model, means that every distributor is helping to take itself and others out of the job market. If I help someone make $20,000 a month, by all standards a great living in America, and she has a number of people on her team who are earning either a full-time or a part-time living, then I know that I'm doing my part to overcome the economic difficulties in this country.

It's a wonderful economic system, and the best part is that I get to work with students of entrepreneurship and teachers of entrepreneurship, and we are all rewarded based on our ability to teach and develop our students.

## CHOOSING A HOME

I want you to apply the principles I've outlined in this chapter even if you're looking to join PartyLite or Amway or Mary Kay. Which brings me to the next obstacle, and a question I'm often asked. You may be a complete beginner, or you may already be self-employed, but it doesn't matter because the same question applies: How do you choose a good network marketing company?

To answer this question I turned to my partner and cofounder at ViSalus, Blake Mallen, who has ten years of experience and has achieved the much-coveted professional multimillionaire entrepreneur status.

Blake broke it down to five simple steps that can be used as a filter, or checklist, when you're doing research on various companies. The first step is choosing a company that has a combination of solid executive management along with network marketing industry experience. Some executives know how to run a business but don't understand the culture of network marketing. Conversely, some multilevel marketing executives don't know how to run a business. "You are looking for a company with a good balance between the two," Blake said. "And a lot of companies in this industry go out of business, so make sure the one you choose has been around for at least three years."

The second step is all about the product or service the company is offering. If you're not passionate about the product you'll be bringing to the market, it's not going to last. Also, the product has to stand on its own. Make sure it's not just moving because a paycheck is attached to it.

The third step is taking a look at the compensation plan. It must be fair, with a way for the person who is just starting out to earn a paycheck for his efforts. Blake said that a lot of plans are designed for the "lotto winner" mentality, for those who are at the top making all the money. A plan is fair when it is fair for the new person who is putting forth the effort and getting paid.

The fourth step is all about the team. You want to answer the question of whether the company is more interested in developing the people, training them, and investing in them than making money. If the answer is no, then that's not a good company. Because as I mentioned before, the most valuable thing you are going to get from becoming a network marketer is the education, so your skills and knowledge can then be translated into anything you do.

And the fifth step is really all about gut instinct: Do you like the people? What kind of culture does the company have? Are these the types of people you can trust and would enjoy being around? Network marketing is most definitely a community, and if you don't align with the culture, you'll be missing out on one of the biggest benefits of the industry.

In this book we talk about having nothing to lose and, indeed, there is very little risk involved with network marketing. This holds true whether you're a beginner, or come from owning a traditional business, or if you're a person who may have just realized that the job market isn't going to get you anywhere very quickly.

I would look at joining a network marketing company as I would any business decision I'd make. Figure out how much it will cost and how long it will take before you can break even. What other benefits will you receive? What does your potential return on capital look like?

When I started ViSalus, I had a very similar conversation with a former pro soccer player named Pete Bunting and his wife, Nicole. Pete was at the time coaching on the side; he'd worked in sales in the past, and his wife had an office job for a cable company. Their income was about $4,000 a month. They were a good-looking, young, vibrant couple with all the potential in the world to make it to the pro level of network marketing.

I have mentored them over the course of the past five years. During that time they've made more than $1,000,000. They've grown as individuals, and now their potential to earn even more is by far their greatest asset. But it wasn't an easy decision. After many long discussions, they scraped together the money to join, which at the time was about $1,000.

I can still recall my first meeting with them at a coffee shop in Riverside, giving them the same key points I've just discussed in this chapter. And I'll tell you the same thing I told them that day, "What do you really have to lose?"

# 15

## LAUNCHING YOUR BUSINESS

---

**W**e often hear the urban legends about how a company was launched. For instance, e-Bay was supposedly founded by a man who wanted to offload his wife's Pez dispenser collection. Google was founded by a couple of engineers working out of their college science lab. The original Facebook was created by a Harvard undergrad as a ploy to gain popularity. We remember these beginnings of great companies whether the stories are true or not. What we don't hear about is the actual systematic approach the founders used to start their businesses.

A business is not a magical thing that you either get right or you get wrong. If you have the right knowledge, the right capital, marketplace opportunity, a passion about your solution, and you follow a formulaic approach to building your business, you have a greater than 90 percent chance of success. Later, when you're telling people about how you started your company, you can forget all these—except for the fact that you started it out of your dorm room.

There are a number of steps for starting a business—choosing a name, business card, Web site, office space, telephone number—yes, all those things are important for launching your business. I used to obsess about these steps, but now that I've achieved a certain level of success and comfort with the process, I would recommend keeping these basics as simple as possible. You can always go back and improve them.

For instance, your company's Web site: every business, no matter how small, no matter what, should have a Web site. If you do not have one, potential clients are going to think you're not capitalized enough. The site can be as simple as one page with a logo, a short description of your business, and contact information. As long as you have something professional on the Web, people will feel secure doing business with you. The same designer whom you hired to work on your Web site may also be able to help you put together a professional-looking logo. Focus on clean lines and a limited number of colors. This makes it simpler to reproduce and gives you a color palette from which you can work when designing the rest of your materials. Think about school colors and sports teams. Two or three colors are able to establish a kind of brand recognition. Try to be consistent with these colors in your advertising, company literature, and labels.

If you can get your head around this important step, then you can start using Facebook, Twitter, and other social media to promote your business immediately. But keep track and build a database; otherwise you'll have no idea who is interested, who is being exposed to your message, and who might be stalking your Facebook page every day just waiting for an opportunity to purchase.

What you want to avoid is thinking that you have to have a fifty-page Web site in order to start doing business. I often did that when I was insecure about the size of my company because I was competing with companies like IBM and Microsoft. I was always trying to make my company look bigger and bigger. And it worked in those times when the use of the Web was new. Someone might take a look at a fifty-page Web site and think, wow, they must be really big. I'm not saying that you can't have a fifty-page Web site, but if your site is big, just make sure your message is very simple.

The trend has changed. Because of savvier consumers, companies are learning to leverage the art of underpromotion. The goal is to be more deliberate and more meaningful. These days, strategically it's just as much of an art not to talk about things as it is to talk about things. And there is a reason for this simplicity: we can no longer retain so much information because we are bombarded by so many sources. For instance, have you ever been in a situation where you recognized a company, but couldn't remember where you were first introduced to it? Did you see its logo in an ad? Was it a Facebook post? Was it on Twitter? Did you see it on someone's T-shirt at a festival? Maybe it was in that damn airplane magazine you got stuck reading because you had nothing else to do during the flight?

Today, the attention span of the end user is so short and so fragmented that you have to first determine how you're going to get them to pay attention to you, and then in that one magic second, how you're going to get them to remember you. Humans can remember lyrics and rhymes, catch phrases and clichés easily. Expressions such as "It is what it is" and "You gotta do what you gotta do" come to mind. We are designed to remember simple repeatable statements. Would this approach to advertising work for your company?

We are moving, as a society, toward buying products and services based on word of mouth. Instead of listening to actors pretending they are having success or enjoyment from using a product, we are buying from friends and listening to recommendations from people we trust. That's why it's so important to make sure your message is repeatable, because not only do your consumers have to buy your product, but they have to be able to explain and recommend your company to their friends in a way that will be easily understood and remembered.

Most action-oriented people don't take the time to think. As you're preparing to launch your business, my advice is that you go away for a week—pitch a tent in the backyard if you have to, but get out of the house—and critically think about how you are going to approach the marketplace. Focus on creating a single solution for a single problem in our society—in the simplest way possible. Consumers want companies to focus on a particular problem, not solve all their problems. Complex, intelligent people like us who start their own companies tend to overthink and overcommunicate our ideas when all the world really wants is a simple solution. Some of the most intelligent people I know are the ones who have learned to make complex concepts simple. If you can apply the "sum up your life in six words" approach to describing the problem your company will solve for its customers, you're golden.

## THAT'S MY STORY, AND I'M STICKING WITH IT

As I said at the start of this chapter, everyone loves an urban legend. Feel free to embrace your own.

Michael Dell built computers in his garage when he was a teenager and started a computer company in his dorm room at UT Austin; now he has an estimated net worth of $12.3 billion. Stories like his grab us because they play to the fantasy of striking out on our own and actually succeeding. Remember, of the millions who dream of doing it, very few people ever actually make that leap into entrepreneurship. Are you an ex-salesperson for IBM who was annoyed at the inefficiencies of certain software, so you invented a product to solve the problem? That's perfect. Are you a stay-at-home mom who was struck by the lack of heirloom-quality children's clothing in your area, so you decided to launch your own boutique? Great—that makes me want to learn more about you and your company.

Keep in mind, too, that you want to make it clear what kind of industry you are in. Give your company a clear identity so its name will become synonymous with the product or service you are offering.

If you're in a direct sales company, you would be creating a team name instead of a company name. For instance, to use an example from ViSalus, one of the distributors named their team the Generational Wealth Builders. They've successfully branded themselves and their team within the company.

Next, create a pitch that helps people understand exactly what your place is within the industry. For example, if you provide standardized-test tutoring for students, the big industry is education, but the specialization is test preparation. Anyone who reads your literature or checks out your Web site should know exactly who your target demographic is—in this case, college-prep students and the parents of those students.

Building off this, you should also make sure that your marketing plan clearly identifies who you are not. Commonly, one of the biggest mistakes new businesses make with their marketing is trying to reach too broadly to capture every possible facet of their industry. While it's great to have broad vision, don't let your company develop an identity crisis.

Use your "what we're not" statement as a positive attribute for creating your brand image. If your business is test preparation, then try including a sentence or two that says, "Ours is a rigorous program designed for focused and intensive SAT/ACT preparation for university-bound students." With that sentence, you are immediately making a statement that identifies your target as students and parents with serious interest and high expectations.

The other thing to consider is your own title within the organization. If you are the founder of the company, it seems logical that you would be the president or CEO. However, you may want to consider bypassing that title until your company becomes a little bit more established. The reasoning behind this is the same for using "we" as opposed to "I" in discussing your company. If you are the only person in your company for the time being, or even if you have a few other employees, a potential client or investor is going to discern very quickly that yours is a very small company; and he or she may make any number of unfair judgments about your company as a result.

Once your company has grown and established solid footing within the market, you should feel free to use whatever title you choose. But in the earliest days, it may be advisable to print a slightly less impressive title on your business cards for the sake of creating a stronger impression.

When I launched 24/7 Tech, I chose the company's name because I thought it conveyed a sense of our mission, which was to provide

around-the-clock service. The domain name was available, so I purchased it immediately and set about designing our Web site. I did a little
research to find out who owned the phone number 877-247-TECH and
was able to negotiate a very cheap deal (under $100) to buy it from the
owner because he was not using it. I went to a design company and had
a logo created for the company.

I was incredibly proud of all of my start-up legwork, but instead of
insisting on the CEO title I had earned, I wanted to be a vice president.
I knew that if I, a young man, walked into someone's office and said I
was the CEO, he or she would know this was a very new and small
operation before I'd even started my pitch. Many clients will be a little
suspicious if the CEO sits down and talks with them at their first meeting, because that implies that the company is either just getting started
and is therefore a risky gamble or that the company is desperate, which
gives the other person all of the power in the negotiations.

However, by the time I'd exited 24/7 Tech and established SkyPipeline, I had a few more years on me, not to mention a lot more experience.
I had a few newspaper and magazine articles to my name, and I had a
reputation as an up-and-coming entrepreneur. Because of that, even
though we were still a small company, I felt I could take over the CEO title
without giving investors the impression that we were too small or too
new to be taken seriously. In reality it was confidence that I needed.

My sales angle was different, too. I made sure that potential clients
understood the positive aspect of working with the company I was heading. At some point in each sales pitch, I'd ask them, "When was the last
time the CEO of AT&T, MCI, or Verizon showed up to actually talk
to you about working on an account with them?" The answer was
always that it never happened, because the companies were too big to
operate that way.

"It's not that they're too big to meet with you," I'd explain. "It's that
they are too big to provide one-on-one, personalized service." I would
give clients my cell phone number and tell them they could call me anytime. That was my first step in assuring them that instead of dealing
with some big corporation that probably outsources its call center, we

would provide customer service unlike anything they had ever had before.

I'm a regular on MSNBC's *Your Business*, a show where they have me stand in an elevator with aspiring entrepreneurs as they pitch me their businesses—"The Elevator Pitch." I am often very surprised at how poorly these entrepreneurs communicate their company's product or service. My advice is that it shouldn't sound scripted or overrehearsed, and that you should have a clear sense of how you want to present yourself, whether you're in an elevator or out making sales calls.

The best elevator pitches get people asking questions. For example, if someone asks me what ViSalus does, I'll say that we market the Body By Vi ninety-day weight-loss challenge, and we've helped hundreds of thousands of Americans lose millions of pounds. Ideally, the person then asks me how it works. And depending on how long the metaphorical elevator ride lasts, I can either continue talking or get the person's contact information and follow up later. You never know whom you're going to meet in an elevator.

## SELL FIRST, ASK QUESTIONS LATER

My final piece of advice for starting your business is to sell first and ask questions later. In other words, if you have a product or service that is ready to go, and you have customers already lining up to purchase it, don't delay until you have every detail spelled out. Go ahead and sell! That's the whole point of everything else you're working on, anyway.

What the owners of most small businesses don't realize is that they can register as sole proprietors and start selling tomorrow. Then you can worry about opening your bank account. With every company I've ever started, the time that I registered it and did all my legal work was when I already had my first check in hand. At some banks, you don't have to be incorporated to open a business account, so I always went and sold the first deal. That forced my hand to actually do all the other work.

Obviously, it's best to have as many things in place as possible before you launch your business, but never let a deal go simply because you don't have things in the order you want them. You can work that out as you go if you need to. Your first sales are something you need to pounce on.

If an entrepreneur showed up at my office looking for advice about how to set all the necessary pieces in place, and he said, "I've got one hundred orders and no idea how to legally incorporate," he's not just someone whom I would want to mentor, he's someone in whom I'd want to invest! This is true for almost any kind of company—service-related companies, shops, and any small business in which the founder has nothing to lose. The possible exception would be someone like an engineer who left Microsoft and who wants to reinvent video on the Web. If it is a product that will take awhile to develop, then obviously you can't start selling right away, although you may be able to begin taking advance orders prior to the product launch.

Not only is the "sell first, ask questions later" approach a solid one, but if you find yourself fortunate enough to be in that position, it also helps eliminate one of the most frustrating remarks that a new entrepreneur often hears: "I don't want to be the first to buy your product. I want to be the second." People want the confidence of knowing they are not stepping into the complete unknown when they make a purchase.

Unfortunately, not everyone is going to be lucky enough to be in such a successful position right off the bat, and you may find yourself faced with the "I want to be the second buyer" attitude. If that is the case, try to craft an answer that addresses the issue while assuaging the fear. For example, if someone asks to see your client list before you have one, you could perhaps answer like this: "Let me tell you about my past work experience and the projects I've worked on to really give you an idea about how my knowledge and understanding are going to maximize this project's effectiveness for you." That lets the potential client know he or she can trust you to do the job because of your relevant experience, and you don't have to come right out and say, "I've never done this before on my own."

You may be asked point-blank, however, if you have any other accounts lined up. If you do not, you need to be honest and tell them that this would be your company's first sale. You can explain how this could actually work to your client's advantage, though, by saying, "We are a new business, and we want you to be our first client. That means we are going to work twice as hard for you. I can offer you a money-back guarantee or whatever it takes to serve you because, as our first client, we'd like to leverage your testimony and help establish our reputation as the hardest-working company in the business. How does that sound to you?" People admire honesty, ambition, passion, and commitment. If you lead with that, people are going to take you seriously.

In the end, as you start your business and take those first steps, you may feel as if the odds are stacked against you. But the truth is that you can successfully navigate your way through the challenges and trials of getting established if you prepare yourself and your business with a smart, calculated marketing plan that will create a buzz around your company, your story, and you as a salesperson, without over promoting yourself. Word of mouth is far and away one of the most effective forms of advertising there is. If you win over your earliest customer with your service, integrity, and hard work, your reputation will precede you as you get deeper and deeper into the market.

Embrace the launch of your business even though it may feel like a fuse has been lit. This is what entrepreneurial urban legends are made of.

# 16

## RAISING MONEY

─────────

I've raised more than $30,000,000 for my companies, and I've invested in many start-ups, and what I've learned is that no idea, no matter how good, and no business plan, no matter how tightly written, will ever get off the ground without funding from somewhere. In chapter 10, "Tap Those Assets," we talked about holding on to your own assets, by using other people's money to get your business started.

Some entrepreneurs I work with don't want the headache of raising capital, so they choose a route that doesn't require fund-raising. If you are one of these types, I completely understand, as it can be all consuming and counterproductive to your business goals. Regardless, securing capital for your business is the make-or-break point. If you can raise the funds you need to start out, you will have all the chance in the world at success. If you can't, you will never get that shot. I've raised as little as $15,000 from an investor and as much as $15 million—and I can assure you that no matter the amount, it is all hard work.

The most important advice I can offer as we begin this discussion is that no matter the source of the money, you have to be willing to earn it. If you aren't willing, then none of what follows in this chapter or this book will be of any use to you because you are not thinking like an entrepreneur.

No matter whom you turn to—whether family, friends, banks, or investors—no one should offer you a dime if you cannot assure them that you will go to your grave trying to earn a return for their money. And if you don't make that promise, probably no one will invest. Keep that in mind as we outline the process, because that will necessarily color everything else that goes into securing investments.

Often, the biggest challenge is knowing where to start. What do you do when you don't have a business—just a business plan—and you're selling an idea rather than a product? How do you start securing those first few investments that give you the momentum to keep going and secure the next possible investor?

I tell everyone to start with their friends and family. This makes sense, of course—they know you, they know your work ethic, and they are probably already familiar with your business plan to some degree.

But you have to be careful. Money issues have strained and ruined countless relationships. If you turn to your relatives or close friends for financing, make sure that the effort you put into making their investment grow is greater than even they could have hoped for. Remember that if you fail to get them their return, it may cost more than just the dollar amount. Just because someone knows your work ethic doesn't mean you can skip over that part of your presentation. Treat interested family and friends as you would any other potential investor. You will probably talk to them differently, of course, but make sure they have the same ironclad promise of your commitment to this project that you would give to a businessperson or a loan officer at a bank.

Tell them the truth. Whenever a company is starting up, there are going to be challenges. There are always going to be rocky patches, even for the most seasoned entrepreneurs. I've had people tell me countless times that my venture was going to fail. Over time, my response to the naysayers has been simple: "If it does fail, I'll be ashamed, but I'll never know it." This always gets a few quizzical looks.

I tell them, "I'll never know about the failure because you will be talking about it at my funeral—I'm going to succeed, or I'll be dead from trying."

Give this same kind of assurance to your relatives. Be sure that your friends have such a level of confidence in you that when they write that check, they know that it is going to be put to the best possible use.

This can be a very risky issue, so proceed with caution. Do not let the terms of your financial agreement become the focus of your relationship. Do not overdiscuss business at family gatherings unless people ask you about it. Do not pressure your friends to invest if they are not completely comfortable with the idea. And don't ask for investments beyond what you know they can afford.

Some of your friends and family are going to think you're crazy for taking these risks, so don't be hurt if they choose not to invest in you. You're going to need emotional support as you launch your business; don't alienate the people who can provide that for you.

For those who do appreciate what you're doing, though, and believe in your business plan, make sure that you pay them back promptly—and first. In other words, you get paid last. Your investors get paid first. Always. From the largest investor to the smallest, they get first dibs at the profits, and you get what is left. After all, you are being paid by the business to manage it.

Probably the number one reason why I am where I am today is because I paid back everybody who gave me money for my businesses. People can look at me and say, "For every dollar I gave him, he gave me five back," or "I gave him a hundred thousand dollars in 2003, and he gave me two hundred thousand in 2004." Big or small, it doesn't matter. You have to look out for your investors first because without them, you have no business and no profits. The return you yield for your investors will pay you dividends forever.

That's how you keep and build relationships when you're asking for money from family, friends, or anyone else. When people see their money come back to them having accomplished something and grown, they see that you are trustworthy and reliable enough to invest in again. If you have a reputation for paying people back, eventually more reluctant investors will be persuaded by your track record and join as well. It's what my mother always told me when I was small: You build relationships by putting others first. You ruin them by looking out only for yourself. Never forget that, especially with investors.

While there are a number of different ways to raise money—debt, common stock, preferred stock—when starting a new business, I usually recommend convertible debt to get started. The way this method works is that you provide your investors with a note stipulating that their investment amount can be either repaid with interest and a premium within a set amount of time (usually a year) or converted to equity in the company at a discount to value of the company at that time, at the discretion of the investor or the company, or by mutual discretion. This instrument can be constructed inexpensively, and it provides flexibility to both parties. I have used this method several times and have also invested in start-ups that initially offered convertible debt.

If your business proves successful, most investors will opt for a share of equity so they can continue to gain returns on their investment. However, the option of repaying the loan in full is an important option to keep on the table if you want to retain complete and total ownership of the company. Even more important, if you find that an investor has proved difficult to work with, you have the option of paying off the loan so that the "difficulty" goes away. From personal experience, I have found that when repaying the loan to end a relationship with investors who were unpleasant, unreasonable, or otherwise a pain in the ass, the interest and the premium were worth every cent.

Recently I made an angel investment of $100,000 in a new company where the terms of my loan were either 20 percent interest repaid within one year or an investment conversion to 30 percent equity in the company. Now, I have to admit that I wouldn't mind holding such a large stake because the company seems to be a very promising one. However, for the sake of the entrepreneurs starting up the business, I hope that they are able to repay me and retain ownership of their work.

If this is your approach, you need to be generous, but not unreasonable, with your interest and equity offerings. The newer your company, the more generous you will have to be because you won't have so much leverage. The deal I just mentioned is highly favorable for me, but I was also their first investor and they were willing to take a bigger risk to secure the large amount of capital they needed to launch their plan.

Common stock and preferred stock get much trickier. Common stock functions just like stock in a publicly owned company does. The gains from it are tied to the company's market value or performance.

Preferred stock is a very complicated instrument. A preferred stock subscription agreement can cost tens of thousands of dollars to create and, if not done correctly, can cost you your company. If an investor will only invest in preferred stock, you should hire a great attorney. As I mentioned in chapter 5, "Seize the Day," this lesson was one of my most expensive early on in my career. I didn't know enough about the rights I had agreed to in my preferred stock agreement. And when the company eventually sold, it cost me millions.

In fact, when we were getting ready to start ViSalus, we first raised about $200,000 in debt and then $1.5 million in preferred stock. We were then able to use some of the proceeds from the preferred stock to pay off the debt. Of course, it took a lot more fund-raising later to get the company where it is today. This was an approach we took only because time and hard experience had helped me to understand how to structure the transaction to meet the needs of all parties.

But how do you land that first big deal? Banks and investors are continuously getting applications and proposals for loans. As we discussed in the last chapter, you have to be able to make yourself and your business plan stand out by offering something unique, superior, or edgy—this is called having points of differentiation.

When it comes to raising capital, though, there is one more aspect that really trumps them all: you have to offer value. I'm not talking about profit potential here, though obviously that is part of the equation. What really makes the first good impression, what helps you to get your foot in the door, is that you demonstrate to the investors the lengths to which you will go to get them a valuable return on their money. And for most people who are in the position to invest, time is their most limited—and, therefore, most valuable—resource.

I learned this lesson early on when I took a gamble and asked to arrange a meeting with one of the founders of Sun Microsystems. I made a five-hour drive from Los Angeles to San Luis Obispo for a very short meeting with him because I wanted his advice. I didn't even pitch to him at that first meeting. I just asked for his advice in launching, growing, and sustaining my new start-up business. But later I knew I could pick up the phone or send him an e-mail to ask, "Could you take a look at this business plan?" because I had first demonstrated to him that I understood how valuable his time was.

Putting forth effort like that is your first step toward demonstrating that you are willing to earn any investment someone might decide to offer you. The advantage of securing one or two larger investors through efforts like this is that those investors can often open the doors to a number of other investors. After all, the goal of any investment is to make a profit, and any investor is going to want your business to grow and succeed. The more investors who are able to offer up capital and expertise, the more rapidly the business can expand its offerings and thus, by extension, its client base, which leads to increased sales and profits.

Therefore, by securing a few "anchor investors" early on, your business will not only have credibility with other venture capitalists, but its networking opportunities are also likely to expand exponentially.

But how can you assure those anchor investors that you are willing to earn their capital? One of the most effective ways is to offer them equity in your company in exchange for their time. This not only shows the investors that you're willing to sacrifice for your company, but it also gives them even more motivation to assist you in making the company profitable because it directly affects their own returns.

When SkyPipeline was still in its early days, Fred Warren agreed to help me raise $1 million to expand it. At the time, my company was doing about $30,000 in sales per month, but we negotiated a deal where he would contribute about one-half of the $1 million I needed, and in the meantime, he would introduce me to a number of other potential investors. Not only did my business grow, but I also benefited from fantastic mentorship from someone who had been in business for years and wanted to make sure that his money, as well as the money of his friends, was being put to good use.

Fred taught me how to be a CEO, but just as important, he introduced me to the Goergen family, who were and still are some of my most valuable contacts. Your reputation with investors is something you will carry with you throughout your career, so guard it well.

Chances are that you will not need nearly so substantial a sum to start your business as I did. But if you are able to make a few key connections and establish credibility with local business leaders, angel investors, or venture capitalists in your area, you may be able to open doors to larger investments as well as smaller ones.

## VENTURE CAPITALISTS: SWIMMING WITH THE SHARKS

I need to offer two warnings to keep in the forefront of your mind when the large investments and/or profits start to roll in. Venture capital relationships are arrangements that are successful only if you are very knowledgeable in how to structure the transaction, if you are smart in choosing whom you work with, and if you are able to keep it all in focus. Surround yourself with the right people who have the right values, philosophies, and intentions with their investments. Whenever money is involved, there is a definite sense of obligation, and you do not want to find yourself in any partnerships with anyone of questionable character, which may not only cause problems in terms of your own alliances and commitments, but it also can hurt your reputation with other, more credible investors.

Additionally, you have to make sure that you keep yourself grounded in terms of how you think about money. It's very tempting, once the profits start rolling in, to think that your days of sacrificing are over. When I sold SkyPipeline as part of a merger, it ended up being a $25 million deal. The newspapers wrote about how I had made so much money as a young kid in my twenties. I had every Wall Street banker calling me. My mom and my friends were all so proud. I thought I had arrived. But I didn't get $25 million in cash. I had been heavily diluted for additional financing rounds, and the actual amount of cash, although significant, would not allow me to retire happily on an island somewhere.

So even though it looked as though I had made a massive windfall, it was a much smaller number than everyone thought—but I kept the story going. I loved that people thought I was a wildly successful multimillionaire, and I started spending as if I were. Whether it is good or bad, society measures you by the watch you wear, the shoes you have on, and the car you drive, and early in my career I invested heavily in that.

Part of maintaining your drive is to try to project confidence at all times, no matter what.

You need to be willing to go out on a limb, set goals, and let your investors see the level of belief you have in your product as well as your ability to sell it. Do not confuse confidence with bravado or self-importance, though. No one wants to be a business partner with someone who is cocky. True confidence is found in the things you don't say and the look in your eyes.

For example, quite often I find myself faced with entrepreneurs who treat my invitation to make their sales pitch as a ploy to steal their ideas. I've had owners of brand-new businesses that have not even launched insist that I sign a nondisclosure agreement before they will agree to speak with me. I don't even know who they are or what their product does, and they are asking me to sign a legal document? And if I balk at signing anything before I at least meet with them, the response I usually get from these entrepreneurs is basically one that accuses me of premeditated theft. If the new product has a patent, as many of them do, the investor will often act as if this is a trump card that gives him or her total legitimacy and commands my respect. In this kind of situation, the request for capital is usually a rather high amount—and again, all for a product that I don't know anything about.

I get dozens of letters from people who basically say, "I have the best idea in the world, and I need you to fund it, but I can't tell you what it is because you might steal it." Not only is that insulting to me personally, but it also demonstrates that the person does not have a grasp of the interpersonal skills needed to raise money, let alone to interact with customers. If he or she has not taken the time to figure out what my motivations, needs, and business practices are, how is this person going to treat a client? I always have to fight the urge to e-mail back, "If your product is so great that I should invest in it sight unseen, then you don't need me because it should be selling itself."

I want to include a quick list of dos and don'ts for pitching to an investor—because as obvious as some of these items may seem, they all address very common mistakes or missteps that can cost you the deal:

- Do turn off your cell phone before the presentation, and do not wear an earpiece.
- Do dress professionally—that means a business suit or a shirt and tie. Casual wear is never appropriate in this kind of setting. There is nothing casual about success.
- Do be sure to ask for the investment at the end of your presentation.
- Do rehearse your presentation a minimum of ten times.
- Don't allow your presentation to run over thirty minutes, and be sure to allow at least fifteen extra minutes for a question-and-answer session at the end.
- Do end the talk by reciting the specific actions that were requested of you.
- Do go back and reread chapter 12, "Million-Dollar Mistakes," before you ask an investor for his or her money.
- Do follow up on everything to which you committed.
- Don't interrupt your prospective investor when he or she is talking.

- Do make sure to answer the investor's question clearly and concisely, and ask him or her after you speak, "Did that answer your question?"
- Don't try to answer questions if you don't know the answer. Say instead, "I don't know, but I will follow up with you on that question."
- Do make sure your investment presentation is printed in color and bound professionally.
- Don't ever respond with negative emotion to a criticism or lack of interest from a potential investor.

You're swimming with sharks; it requires a delicate balance of persuasiveness but not pressure, extreme sacrifice but not self-destruction, and great confidence and genuine humility. Raising capital is probably going to be the most difficult part of establishing your business. You must be willing to work yourself to the very brink to secure each investment and then continue to work yourself to the brink to make sure you get a return. And if you forget everything else I've written in this chapters, ask for the order and close the investor.

# 17

## GROWING, HIRING, AND FIRING

---

**O**ne night a few months ago I had an after-hours party at my penthouse. The music was loud, and there were about a hundred people—models, celebrities, and old friends—all celebrating the decadence of our times. As I've mentioned, I like to entertain, so I was indulging in one of my favorite rituals with the guests: leading them around on a tour, explaining each piece of art. I turned the corner and suddenly I saw a nightmare from the past: one of the most evil criminals from my old neighborhood, an OG from my gang, was standing in my living room. It had been fifteen years since I had last seen him, and he had the same look on his face, the look of a man with nothing to lose.

My first thought was, "I'm getting robbed. Or killed." My next thought was, "Where's my security?" But I knew they were no match. If this guy was there on a mission, no security, armed or not, would stop him. Carlos weighs about 280 pounds—he's a massive guy. Last I'd heard he was serving time in prison for stabbing someone in the liver. He's a complete psycho. This was not the type of person I wanted hanging around my life today. I had no choice but to ask him what he was doing there. The first thing he said was, "Your homeys are all proud of you."

By coincidence Carlos had been out partying in Hollywood that night and overheard some people talking about heading over to a party at Ryan Blair's house. He recognized my name and decided to follow them in.

This was the guy who had recruited me and jumped me into the gang. This is the guy who had beaten me up and ordered many of the crimes we committed. I was literally staring my past in the face.

One of my friends came up to me as I was standing there talking to Carlos, and I said, "You'll never guess who this is." After I explained who the thug standing in my living room was, my friend turned to Carlos and asked, "Why would you recruit Ryan?" Then he looked at me as if to imply, "This pretty-boy white kid."

Carlos said, "Ryan was an insecure kid. He'd just lost his father and would do anything to be accepted, and he was the perfect kid to do my dirt."

In essence, he'd understood my psychology. I was the right age, the right socioeconomic status, and I had the right upbringing. I was the perfect person to get the job done. Carlos had developed a profile for the best recruit for the job he needed done, and when he met that recruit, he gave him the job.

Maybe it's a strange example, but hearing his words as he described why he'd recruited me made me realize that I use the same technique when I'm hiring someone for my company. I am looking for the right type of person to get the job done.

In order to grow your business, you have to recruit and hire, just as Carlos did to grow his gang. On the streets you have to recruit new members frequently because you have high turnover, and the gangs that were the most successful were always building their numbers. It's the same in business. I've seen companies fail because they didn't hire people when they should have; I've also seen businesses suffer because they hired the wrong persons (see chapter 12, "Million-Dollar Mistakes"). The best advice I can offer as you start the hiring process is to know, just as Carlos did, what kind of employee you are looking for.

In most cases, in a small business making its first few hires, you're not looking for a person with highly specialized training but someone who can do a little bit of everything—a jack-of-all-trades. You need someone who will be willing to work the phones, take out the trash, interact with customers, and mop the floor—in other words, anything that will allow you more time to make sales or craft the company's strategy.

You need to make sure that the person you hire is willing to accept that kind of position. Some people are adamant about what they are and are not willing to do as part of a job. If someone thinks dusting the shelves or refilling the paper towel dispenser in the bathroom is beneath him, don't hire him.

The first position I've filled in any of my businesses has always been that of office manager. In fact, that was usually how I listed the job when I advertised it. I wanted someone who was interested in managing with a sense of responsibility, because that would indicate a personal connection to the company. In each interview, I would look for someone who would take the initiative, someone who would be on the lookout for whatever job might need doing. That kind of person tends to take pride in her work, which is exactly the kind of attitude I wanted in my company.

When you are ready to hire for highly specialized positions, you should keep this kind of attitude in mind. Employees need to have a defined job description and a clear set of expectations, but you should also explain that from time to time they may be called upon to step outside of their job descriptions to help with a project or situation that is important to the company.

People who are overly protective or territorial about their job descriptions tend not to be team players. You want someone who is concerned with doing good work for the sake of the customer, product, brand, and company, not someone who is just hacking away at a job strictly for a paycheck.

I've always believed that my most valuable asset is the quality of the people I've been able to attract and recruit for my companies. If you surround yourself with tremendous talent, you will find yourself challenged and stretched to levels you never imagined. It is my goal to be in awe of every person I hire. I want to see traits in her or him that are more dynamic or more positive than my own abilities in that area, because I know that simply by working with that person, I will be able to grow and the company will prosper, thanks to this continuous reach for improvement.

I've seen entrepreneurs stunt their growth because they were afraid to hire people smarter than they were. Bill Gates once said in an interview that the secret to his success was that he hired people smarter than he was, and he's pretty smart. Good people don't take a job just for salary. They take a job for camaraderie, learning opportunity, or because of their career direction. As the CEO, your job is to clearly articulate those elements you offer your employees that are not money oriented, so that you can attract the best of the best talent without necessarily having to pay the highest wages. In almost every great company I have studied, the elements that recruited the candidates were what led to that company's greatness. And in every failed company I've studied, it was a lack of attention to those elements that led to its failure.

At ViSalus, we spent so much time building the field sales culture that now we find ourselves shifting gears to work on building the internal employee culture, so we can grow our company into a great one. I didn't pay much attention early on to the employee culture because I was focused on building the sales culture in the field. The sales culture is responsible for the current growth, and the salespeople should be greeted as heroes because they're the ones generating the revenue that pays everyone else's salary, but the one thing that could stop the rate of growth at this point is not building the employee culture to complement the sales culture. I've seen some businesses in my industry fail because employees and management actually grow to hate the very people who are generating the revenue.

As ViSalus grew from $36 million in sales in 2010, to $231 million in sales in 2011, to more than $600 million in sales in 2012, we went from having roughly fifty employees to over 450 employees. We expanded with card tables, piling people on top of one another because we were growing so fast we didn't have space for them. I realized that if I didn't focus on our culture, before long we'd end up hiring the wrong people, so I relocated to Detroit, where ViSalus is headquartered, and started the process of building a new facility specifically designed to create the culture that would attract great employees. A lot of CEOs talk about culture, and in most cases that's all they do—talk. You can observe culture in action but the best way to impact culture is by changing how your employees experience it. We spent more than $10 million on our Detroit facility, and we didn't spend it on the "e-suite" office walls and ivory towers; we spent it on technology—like our employee kitchen, lounges, gym, work utilities, and tools—that would keep our employees connected to the pulse of our customers and with each other. Create a culture that will attract "A-players," then A-players will attract other A-players, and eventually your employees will break bread and make bread together.

I know some of you are reading this and are thinking, "I have only four employees, why does culture matter?" I can tell you from experience that I wish I'd started focusing on culture earlier in my companies. When your company's culture gets away from you, you feel alienated until you no longer feel like it's your company—and that's when most entrepreneurs decide to sell out, or get fired by their board of directors, or any number of other horror stories that happen when the wrong culture is accidently created.

As an angel investor I drive home the importance of culture, even with start-ups. A prime example is Fragmob, a small software start-up created by my friend Jade Charles. As chairman of his board, I insisted that he define cultural values and find the attributes of people he wanted to work with for the rest of his life (A-players), even as he was hiring his second and third employees. It went totally against the grain for a software-engineering company to focus on culture, not code. Today, Fragmob is a multimillion dollar company, and both its founder and its board are very happy that he listened to me.

In late 2011 I started to hate the culture of ViSalus. We were making errors, launching products that sucked and sometimes even had to be trashed. Our employees were acting entitled because of our success, not grateful for it. It was so bad that I had no choice but to step in and make some serious changes. I fired some people and sat down with my team to create a set of core values for our culture, core values that we aspire to today.

These values aren't just some mission statement you write on a wall. I hate that kind of thing. These values are used to reward positive behavior and to help correct negative behavior, and are so important to us that every hiring and firing decision is made based on how a person connects to them. These values create a culture, a common language, and when properly executed touch all of the five senses:

1. Be inspired. Be inspiring. *We are part of a movement that inspires people to achieve incredible health and financial transformations every day. Be proud that you are part of the team that makes this possible, and inspire others through your actions to be more, do more, and make a difference.*

2. Build trust through collaboration. *Use a collaborative team spirit to earn the trust of others, and trust your team in return. Be authentic and transparent in your communications, and trust in your team to recognize your victories and pull together to overcome your challenges.*

3. Be a good teacher and a better student. *The best teachers are the best students, and every person at every level of our Community can be both. You are here because of your talents, and teaching others what you know lifts our collective ability to serve. Be eager to learn, unafraid to ask why, and relentless in pursuit of knowledge.*

4. Think like an entrepreneur; be resourceful. *ViSalus champions entrepreneurship, and our best team members will be able to take the Challenge Promoter's perspective in all aspects of their role. Think about what a Promoter needs to best serve a customer and how you can help them in that pursuit. Also, think like a business owner. If your role were its own company, what decisions would*

*you make to serve your customer, increase profits, and go the extra mile?*

5. Challenge yourself. *Join the rest of the ViSalus Community in setting goals, reaching for those victories, and celebrating those who cross the finish line. Whether it is a personal health goal or simply digging deeper to achieve more in your role, avoid complacency and always strive for more. What more could you do if you challenged yourself, and how good would it feel to achieve that goal?*

6. Seek simplicity. *Less is more.*

At ViSalus, we don't hire for skill and experience—we hire for culture. Skill and experience get you a call back; culture gets you a career. As Zappo's CEO Tony Hsieh says, "Your culture is your brand."

A great company is the sum of its great people.

Early on in my career, I couldn't fathom hiring people who were more expensive than I was, but one time a venture capitalist, realizing I was weak in the finance area, required that I hire a world-class CFO at a rate significantly higher than I was making. It was humbling, but I knew this individual was the best person for the job, and I looked at it as an investment in the growth of our company. I never regretted that decision.

One of our board members, Bob Dilworth, told me that when he was CEO of Zenith, his top salespeople made significantly more than he did. I was shocked. "They make twice as much as you," he told me. "That's when you know you got it right."

Many of our distributors at ViSalus make several million dollars a year, and there is no employee, including myself, who makes anywhere near that. As CEO, you have to remember that all of these talented, well-compensated people are building your equity and your profits, and that contributes to your compensation.

If you're worried about how much you make a year as a business owner compared to what your employees are making, you're being employee minded. You need to be entrepreneurially minded and create a culture in your company that is also entrepreneurially minded. To maintain that kind of chemistry, you have to be very selective about whom you bring aboard. A person who brings a condescending air, any kind of laziness, or a hostile attitude to the group can completely destroy the positive atmosphere you've worked so hard to create.

When I worked for my stepfather, I watched his business struggle because he continuously brought on the cheapest help he could hire, whether the people fit with his established team or not. He never took the time to screen for the right attitude, work ethic, or personality that would accentuate and add to the talent he already had in his company. As a result, the company never grew beyond my stepfather's talents, simply because he never brought on anyone more talented than he was.

In my effort to build the best teams in the world, I sat down with Coach John Wooden to learn how he picked his starting five. He wasn't into recruiting the hottest, most headline-grabbing players out there; instead, he researched each potential recruit carefully to learn how that player would fit in with his team. When he or his assistants went on visits, they would carefully observe the young man's behavior, not only toward his teammates but toward his parents—was he respectful? They would look to see how he interacted with the maintenance staff—did he quickly move out of the way when someone was mopping the court, or did he make the person work around him? How did he leave his area of the locker room—was it a mess he expected someone else to handle, or did he take responsibility for his own belongings and clean up after himself?

All of these factors were part of the recruiting process for Coach Wooden because he wanted to make sure that he was going after only the players who would enhance the chemistry of the UCLA basketball team rather than break it down with a negative attitude or disruptive personality.

I really take this lesson to heart when I prepare to hire someone. As I write up the position posting, I try to take a similarly thoughtful approach about what kind of person I want to recruit for my team. I think the way Philip did when he was recruiting me, and I define the candidate's characteristics, including history, personality, and what drives her or him; then I tailor the ad around that image.

I want to have as clear a picture as I can of the people I intend to bring on board. I want to know what schools they went to and why they chose those schools. I want to know how they view themselves, how they interact with others, how they perceive their role within the company. I really want to understand the personality, motivation, and worldview of each person I hire because those are the characteristics that will affect everyone else in the company.

Obviously, you would not hire someone based on things like political views or religious beliefs. Not only is that a violation of nondiscrimination laws, it is also unethical. You have to be careful not to ask too many personal questions regarding age or family status. You may think that you are simply being friendly, but it will be worth your time to do a little research to determine what kind of specific questions are and are not legally permitted as part of an interview.

But you do want to make sure that you evaluate your applicants based not only on their capabilities but also on how their personalities will fit in with the company. You want new employees to be comfortable with the ones already on staff and to be able to blend with them in a way that not only complements what you've already got but also gives the new hires a chance to exercise their unique skill sets, talents, or perspectives.

## THE CONNECT FOUR TECHNIQUE

One screening technique I use is the Connect Four board I keep on my desk. I will often challenge a potential applicant to play me in a round, which enables me to observe a number of things about the person. Not only do I see how she calculates strategy, but I also get a chance to learn about her level of competitiveness and sportsmanship. If a person has a chance to beat me and chooses not to take it, I am not interested in bringing her on board. I want someone who isn't afraid to challenge me and is willing to assert her point of view if it will result in the most favorable outcome. Likewise, if someone is a poor sport by being overly competitive and taking a loss badly, or by becoming overly aggressive during the game and gloating after a win, I don't want that person as part of the team. All the mentors and business leaders I have spoken with have cited the quality of their teams as the reason for their success. Nothing is worth risking that team balance.

I often take my executives on trips to other companies to study their cultures, and one company I have visited often is Zappos. During a Q&A session with Tony Hsieh, I asked him how he makes hiring decisions, because at the time I had hundreds of jobs open and had failed on a few recent hires. What he taught me was simple, yet profound. He said, "If you wouldn't go camping with the person for a week, don't hire them."

This is the ultimate "smell test" to reinforce the gut instincts you're going to use when choosing your employees. Would they keep the fire going or worry about the dirt under their nails? Are they going to complain about their accommodations? Would they leave trash all over the campsite? Would they carry their own weight? I took Tony's camping analogy literally, and now I take many of my team members to the extreme environment of Burning Man every year. At the end of a trip to Burning Man you'll know whether you want to work with someone.

You've heard me talk about "A-players" in this book. In order to get A-players you need to define the attributes you are looking for. The people I want to hire are: loyal, passionate, smart, ambitious, optimistic, personally invested in their work, curious, original, collaborative, competitive, adaptable, resourceful, high energy, inspiring, and influential.

Now does that sound like someone you could spend a week with in the desert?

For me, commitment and loyalty are incredibly important. If the employee seems to jump from job to job to job, continuously chasing the bigger, better deal, I'm not interested. Sometimes, of course, a person has several "blips" on his résumé as a result of something else, so I want to make sure to give him a fair shake if he meets the qualifications. But I'm always on the lookout for people who match my image of how the ideal job candidate will act.

You need to go with your gut when making hiring decisions. If the person just doesn't feel like the right fit, she probably isn't. Trust your instincts in this regard—I've ignored mine in the past and made some horrible hiring choices that cost millions. Put a price tag on a new hire: Is it worth the $50,000 or $100,000 if she becomes a fully productive employee? What if the employee doesn't work out? How much will it end up costing you if this is the wrong person once you take into account salary costs, disruption in the office, lost sales, advertising for and rehiring someone new? Often, hiring the wrong person can be a hundred-thousand-dollar-plus mistake.

Look for warning signs that the candidate might represent your company in a negative light with clients. Some of the worst mistakes I've made in hiring have come when I ignored my instincts and hired someone who seemed careless or not genuinely interested in the company. I have hired people who were overly casual, who used slang or even crass language in interviews. That kind of oversight has always proved to be a mistake. I also pay attention to whether candidates speak negatively about former coworkers or bosses. Sometimes, though, I have rationalized hiring a person who goes against the professional traits I hold so important, and it has always come back to haunt me.

Luckily, there are a few ways to rectify hiring mistakes. One is by relocating the person to a different area in the company. For example, if I hire someone to handle my customer accounts and I find that his job skills really aren't a good match for that position, I can simply restructure his position if he is a good worker whom I would like to keep with the company. I can look to see if there is a better match for his talents or experience somewhere else in the company, so that I can retain his talent and loyalty but in a position that both of us will probably be happier with. Maybe he is better at operations; if so, I can slide him over there and start looking for a new customer accounts manager.

If, however, the person simply does not fit in with your company, and he or she is detrimental to your team, you need to let that employee go immediately. It's not pleasant, and it's not easy, but it is necessary to fire people—and you need to get comfortable with that reality very quickly. I've hired and fired hundreds of people, and I have learned that you have to look at the chore as a necessity for the life of your business.

Firing is one of the most important things for a growing business. You should think of it like pruning a plant—you don't want its resources to continue to go toward branches and leaves that aren't producing. Instead, you need to trim them off right away so the finely manicured result is something that maximizes its resources in the most effective way for the overall health of the organism. Similarly, you need to cut out the wrong people quickly. A bad employee is a cancer for your company that spreads and damages the entire body. The sooner you remove the problem, the better.

You need to call the employee into your office and explain how he or she is not living up to the expectations of the position. It is incredibly helpful to have available job evaluations from supervisors or even ones you've personally completed in which you have expressed your displeasure in the individual's performance on previous occasions. It is important that you communicate with your employees so that they know what they need to improve before the ax falls.

If you have had a frank and honest evaluation of your employee's performance previously, you will have had the chance to explain, "When I hired you, I thought you were the right fit for this job; but since then, I have come to see that your [communication skills or work ethic or attitude or judgment] is not up to par. If things do not improve, I will have to let you go for the sake of the company." By communicating your expectations to employees before the point of needing to fire them, you are not only giving them an opportunity to change their ways, but you are also making sure you have a clear record of their poor performance should they choose to challenge your decision to finally let them go.

Ask yourself a question about each employee. If he came to you and said, "I am leaving your company for a new opportunity," what would your gut reaction be? Would you be devastated because this person's contribution is invaluable and irreplaceable, or would you be happy because by leaving, he would eliminate many problems and open up an opportunity for someone more qualified? This is a lesson I learned from Jim Collins's excellent book *Good to Great: Why Some Companies Make the Leap . . . and Others Don't*, and it has proved invaluable.

One of the key ways to align your company with its employees is to align their compensation to the company's objectives. Always remember this simple truth: compensation drives behavior. As you hire employees, think carefully about how you'll compensate them. For my executives I create MBO programs, which stands for "management by objectives." In my call center, I might give the workers a commission for every upsell they make. With my outbound call center, I give them a commission for every customer they win back. My event team receives bonuses if the event hits the quality mark and is on budget. If an employee is doing a good job and the company is growing, I like to reward that person.

I have seen many businesses where the owners are getting rich, but the employees' salaries are stagnating. You don't want that. It creates a morale problem. You want your employees aligned with the objectives of the company, so that every one of you is moving in step toward your goals. You have to give a clear path to compensation.

If your assets are limited, you may find yourself looking for someone with less experience who will not expect so high a salary. On the other hand, you may be willing to pay a higher price to bring on board someone with a proven track record and relevant experience and education. Sometimes you will find a great combination: someone who has experience but is looking for part-time work or who is willing to take a pay cut to be in a job she or he will love.

You should always strive to pay fair, market-based wages to recruit and maintain talented, reliable, and loyal employees. I have also incentivized my employees with equity if I want them to be long-term team members with the company. There are multiple ways to issue equity. You can do stair-step vesting, where one earns an increasing amount each year he or she remains with the company. You can do cliff vesting, which means that if an employee stays to a certain point, he or she gets the full amount of an agreed-upon percentage, but forfeits everything if he or she leaves before that point.

You can also do vesting based on deferring market rate wages, which can be a prime way to hire top wage earners if you're not quite in a place to afford them. If someone is worth $100,000 but you can only pay $75,000, you can offer deferred compensation wherein you draw up a contract guaranteeing that when the company hits $50 million (or whatever your goal is), the employee will make ten times his deferred income for each year he has stayed with you. This means, for example, that for the employee who defers $25,000 per year and stays with your company for, let's say, four years (when you meet your goal), he could potentially earn $25,000 × 10 × 4 years = $1 million! I used this technique at both SkyPipeline and ViSalus. In fact, I once used this deferred compensation plan with my entire start-up team. One executive earned more than $300,000 by deferring a mere $25,000 in wages.

There are three forms of compensation that all employees should earn. The first is money, the second is recognition, and the third is contribution. To have a strong team, you need to be paying your employees with all three.

My first taste of compensation through contribution was at a Sky-Pipeline holiday dinner, when I looked around at all the children who were laughing and playing and having a wonderful time. And then it hit me—I have a responsibility to them. I have a personal responsibility to keep this company up and running and generating business because that is what is putting food on their tables at home, what is buying them school supplies and warm clothes for the winter. Reminders like that can be tremendous motivators that give perspective and meaning to the other forms of compensation you'll receive while building your business. I receive compensation from contributing to my employees, and you will want your employees to receive the same feeling of contribution as a result of their service to their customers.

Just remember that your product is more than simply the goods or services you have to sell. Your product is your people—how they represent your company, how they interact with clients, how they view their own professional lives. And this is a direct result of whom you recruit and how you treat your people. You want the highest-quality product you can offer to give your customers the best value. Be sure you think about your employees in the same way by offering them a solid team of peers within the company and the right kind of incentives to keep them excited, active, and content. The only thing that separates you from greatness is the people you hire. No great company has ever been created without great people. And when you come across a great potential person for your team, get creative and start selling. The following is the e-mail I used to close the deal when I hire the former president of Herbalife to be the president of ViSalus. The problem was he was rich and happily retired. I needed to find another way to get him to join our company.

After a few e-mails and an in-person meeting, I really liked John. I thought he was the perfect fit for what we were looking for. When the perfect fit shows up, you need to sell that person on your company, just as you would an investor, and as you'll see below, I was selling:

Subject: Re: Vi-President-Job Description

Date: Wed, 6 Jan 2010 19:54:22-0800
From: ryan@visalus.com
To: john-purdy

Thanks for the reply John. I think you're the right fit. . . . 5 years
from now if we do what I think we can, . . . you'll be sending
your daughter off to a school . . . Where dad's on the board :).

I'll be coaching little league for my 6 year old. . . . We'll both
be happy we made the decision.
My personal opinion is you've got this in you. Done selling. Ryan

His response was:

From: John Purdy

Sent: Thursday, January 07, 2010 7:17 AM
To: Ryan Blair
Subject: RE: Vi-President-Job Description

I love your style!! I like the picture.
John
ps She wants to go to Juilliard in NYC!!!!!!! I guess I had better
go back to work

He did go back to work and did provide significant value to ViSalus. As your company grows, you're going to need a number of key hires. So I ask you: Who's the one person you need to take your company to new heights? Who's your perfect recruit?

# 18

## CASHING OUT

----

There will come a point in your company's life when you are faced with a tough decision: Should you stay on with the business you've built, or is it time to move on and cash out?

It is a serious and deeply personal decision that no one else can make for you. In this chapter, I want to lay out the various scenarios and possibilities to consider when you do find yourself faced with this choice, and I will suggest things you should consider if you find yourself inclined toward making an exit. I've made and sold lots of stock in my time and have been on both sides of the deal—the guy writing the check and the guy getting one written to him. Here are some key things to think about before you take money off the table.

Phil Jackson, coach of the Los Angeles Lakers, loved to say, "Every life has a cycle, and too many people stay on longer than they should, and they actually reduce the value of what it is they've accomplished." Now that you have gone from being unemployed or unhappy in your job, how do you know when the time is right for you to finish the game and celebrate what you've accomplished—and how do you exit the court gracefully?

As you begin considering the future, you will need to evaluate the various options open to you. The three most important are timing (Is this the best time for me to leave the company?), direction (In what direction do I see both my company and the industry headed?), and opportunity (What options are out there right now that are worth more examination as potential means for an exit?).

Timing can be both a subjective issue and an objective one. In the first case, consider your health and energy, other dreams you want to pursue, family issues, a desire to retire to another part of the country—any one of these could affect how you view the issue.

When the thrill of the entrepreneurial spirit is gone from your company, and you've maximized the potential of your industry because you have a comfortable and solid market share, you may be interested in selling to pursue other business ventures. Maybe you want to explore a different industry, or you find yourself intrigued by new ideas. Green business, for example, is highly valuable right now, and perhaps you are interested in trying your hand at developing a technology that reduces carbon footprints while the timing is right. Whatever the case, this kind of restlessness is very common among entrepreneurs because of the innate competitive nature that drives many of us to this field in the first place. My venture capitalist friends call this founder's syndrome, when it's time for the founder(s) to move on.

On the other hand, the timing might be right or less than ideal. For example, a person looking to sell his home construction business in Southern California would have made a killing if he had sold it in 2007. If you know that the market is at a high in your field, that might affect your decision. Conversely, that same individual would have a much more difficult time selling his business in 2009, simply because of the downturn in the market. If your industry is currently in a slump, that can also alter your perspective on whether now is the right time to leave.

This also points to the next factor you need to consider: direction. Are you in tune with the markets? Do you have a sense of which way the trends are starting to point? For example, after several years of growing and developing SkyPipeline, it became clear to me that cell phone companies were going to give us a run for our money. I didn't want to be in the business of trying to fight that, and neither did my investors. I know that there are some people who relish that kind of challenge, but I felt that I wanted to explore other options to go along with the new direction of the industry rather than carve out a niche contrary to it, so I began looking for buyers. We reached out to a few of our competitors and asked whether there was an interest in combining our businesses. Two emerged, and we successfully sold the company to the higher-bidding competitor.

Even if the industry itself is not headed in a direction you want to avoid, you may find that it is time for the company to take a new direction—and that you are not the person best suited to do that. Perhaps you no longer feel you can contribute as a founder the way you once did or that your research indicates that it is better for your company to diversify or specialize. Maybe that type of shift doesn't play to your strongest skills, but you have a person in mind who would be an ideal leader. It could be that now is the time to hand over control to a new CEO who can take what you've established and build and grow your company to new heights.

Finally, you will want to consider the various opportunities that are out there. If you have someone with a generous buyout offer right now, you may want to take a serious look. Do you want to hand over the company to someone who cares about it, knows the business, and is willing to pay you a premium that will make the years you invested in it seem worth it?

You should also be looking ahead toward other opportunities that may be coming down the pike so you can prepare your company. For example, if you know that Microsoft will probably begin trending toward a certain area over the next twenty-four to forty-eight months, and your company has an effective product in that market, you may want to begin to position your company to be appealing to Microsoft as they look to absorb smaller businesses that can meet that particular need. We will discuss in the following pages how to begin aligning your company so you are poised for an offer.

If you do determine that the time is right for you to leave, you can't simply walk out the door one day and be done with it, though. You need to have an exit strategy that sets your business up for a smooth transition and a successful future. If nothing else, you owe that to your stakeholders.

The first way to exit is probably the most appealing to a majority of people, and that is to retire while maintaining an interest that continues to earn you money. It's commonly referred to as golden handcuffs—a play on the golden parachute idea for big-name CEOs leaving with huge severance packages. Whether you have a home-based business or twenty-five franchise locations, golden handcuffs are a permanent tie to your company that bring you residual profits while keeping you close enough to the business for you to give advice, meet with shareholders, and go over corporate affairs as the need arises.

In many cases this isn't an exit but is rather a method for getting a good team to run the company under your supervision for the long term. To some people, this isn't appealing—when they retire, they want a clean separation. For other people, this is the perfect arrangement that allows them to enjoy the benefits of what they've created while also allowing them to stay active in the business they love. This is also a good system for maintaining the confidence of investors or shareholders, who are often spooked by a complete handover of power. By retaining a presence within the company, albeit a limited one, you can help ease fears of the unknown and still add value to the enterprise.

For this kind of exit to be successful, though, you have to make sure that you have left the books in order and that you have appointed the right people to whom you will hand over the reins of leadership as you move toward a lesser role. We'll discuss more about this later on.

The second way to exit is through a merger or acquisition. In other words, if there is an interested person or group who wishes to purchase the business from you at a fair price, it may be an offer worth considering. Likewise, if another company makes an offer to fold yours into its own operations, you may also have a good opportunity to leave, while knowing that your years of effort will carry on, and your employees will have continued stability. A merger or an acquisition can be a very complicated transaction. I've been on the buying side a few times as well as on the selling side. SkyPipeline merged with NextWeb, which was bought by Covad Communications. Fusion merged with ViSalus and was bought by Blyth. PathConnect was merged with Solution X and the code we wrote went on to become the core behind Solution X's Unity product. We then sold Solution X to Icentrix and now our technology powers millions of direct sellers and is a $15 million-plus business. I have been a part of several merger and acquisition deals and, fingers crossed, might one day find myself on the buyer or seller side again.

Your final option is to take the company public (IPO) so that shareholders—in addition to you—become the owners. In this scenario, rather than selling to one party, you are selling part of the company to anyone who wants to own a share, and you are allowing it to be traded on the stock exchange. In the interest of full disclosure, I should tell you that I have never taken a company public. At ViSalus, we were seriously considering taking our company public on the London Stock Exchange in late 2007. We had a term sheet from a billion-dollar hedge fund to help with that move, but after careful consideration, we decided to sell to Blyth. And then in August 2012, we were again looking at going public. This time we had 450 percent growth for the first half of the year and Blyth behind us, not to mention a world-class management team, prominent investment bankers and analysts, and a team of high-powered attorneys all lined up. We'd filed our S-1, and just as we were preparing for the roadshow, I decided not to go public.

It was one of the most difficult decisions I've had to make—one that meant I'd have to scrap all those 100-hour work weeks and millions of dollars invested, and sacrifice the vision I'd painted for our Promoters about being part of a public company all in one "should we go, or no" moment. Not to mention it significantly decreased Blyth's share value, and being a large shareholder of Blyth myself, it cost me greatly in the short term as well. That's the problem with the public markets—they are short-term. We were just days away from the election and the market was uncertain about our industry and the economy as a whole, and because of that uncertainty our perspective value was reducing by the minute. It wasn't the right time, and had we proceeded with the IPO it would have hurt ViSalus, not helped it as we had planned. We had a number of stars align for us to go public, but the markets just weren't there for us, or our industry for that matter.

As a CEO, your job is to do what's best for the company, not for yourself. I knew taking a company public in an uncertain market would have put tremendous pressure on operations, devaluing all the hard work our team had done to build ViSalus and detracting us from building a world-class brand. So no matter how emotionally or financially invested I was, in the end it was a difficult, yet simple, decision. And, as I've said before, focus is saying "no." We needed to focus on building ViSalus in the long term, not selling shares in the short term.

When I was leaving SkyPipeline, we first merged with another small company called NextWeb, then sold our combined equity to Covad, which was a public company. At the time I made my exit, the stock was trading at about $0.70 a share, and when I sold my shares, they were about $2.60 each. Many of my investors followed suit and made up to five or six times their initial investment because of our exit plan and strategy; others chose to remain invested in the company and saw the company go through some difficult times before it was eventually bought for $1.05 per share. Those investors didn't yield the same return as those of us who took our money off the table. My responsibility was to get them liquidity so they could determine how much money they wanted to make, and that was exactly what we did. It ended up being a good strategy for the business because I couldn't develop it the way it needed to be developed, but NextWeb/Covad had the means and the interest to do just that. My investors could then decide for themselves whether they wanted to align with the new company or move their interests elsewhere.

From a financial point of view, the golden handcuffs solution is almost always the most preferable form of cashing out because it leaves the greatest number of assets in your name, which translates to greater profits—not just during your lifetime but as part of your estate. Mergers and acquisitions are never easy, with their legal wranglings and contract terms. They also can potentially endanger the jobs of some of your employees who may be let go because their positions duplicate those that already exist in the other company. This is called consolidated savings, and it is a common practice to buy a company with an eye toward consolidation. Also, a company's bid to go public may not be successful. ViSalus' attempt was not. I know many public company CEOs who wish that they were with private companies because of the challenges that a public company brings. I can tell you for sure in hindsight that we made the right decision not to go public in the fall of 2012.

But each situation is different, and if a merger will open new markets for your product, it may end up being the wisest option. Or if you feel that the investment potential of a publicly traded company is what your business needs to reach the next level, then these might be the right choices for you after all. Seek counsel from board members and advisers who have been through these very complex processes and . . .

## LAWYER UP

If you want to take the route of offering your company for sale, you will probably have a number of different options for marketing your company. There are business brokers and investment bankers who specialize in how to approach the potential buyers for your business. You may also find yourself talking to local competitors, as we will discuss a little later on. Whatever the case, when you are involved in selling your company, the most important thing you can possibly do is hire a good lawyer to pore over the details and negotiate the best possible contract. In the first ViSalus/Blyth transaction, we spent more than a million dollars on attorneys to ensure that the right deal was reached for both parties.

When ViSalus sold to Blyth in 2008, the contract was ninety-six pages of legalese. I remember spending hours on the phone reviewing every line of every page with all of the deal's team: our attorneys, our executive board, and our management team. We had people on the line from New York, Philadelphia, Miami, and Los Angeles, and we read over every single word of that contract. That is what we had to do, because it literally meant millions to each of us. And it turned out that one term, *flex year,* was the most important term in the entire contract. (It gives us the option to push the buyout back a year, and we used it to get through the recession.) That contract was worth $792.7 million; how's that for apples?

Unfortunately, many entrepreneurs make the mistake of thinking, *I hired the lawyer to write that contract for me; I'm not going to read every word of it, that is their job.* That's the biggest mistake you can possibly make in an exit. During the ViSalus transaction, I was trying to push through the agreement when Todd Goergen stopped me and, almost yelling, said, "Ryan, we are going to read every single word, every word, on this call." There were ninety-six pages, one hundred words a page, and six people on the call—it took more than four hours. But that was an important lesson for which I am grateful, because I learned that you have to make sure you understand every detail of the deal so you know where you stand, where your employees stand, and where your company stands after the deal is finalized. Don't be afraid to stop the meetings and ask questions. Sometimes the concepts are very complex, and only the pros in the room will fully grasp them. Make sure you understand everything, and don't be too intimidated to ask, "What does that mean to me, specifically?" In one deal, I stopped the meeting several times to ask questions, saying, "I am not familiar with this concept and how it applies. Will you please explain it to me in detail?" Truth be told, sometimes I knew exactly what they were talking about, but I wanted to make sure everyone in the room understood it, too. Either way, it is your job to make sure you and your team fully understand everything to which you are agreeing.

I want to insert a note here on the importance of making sure your employees are well taken care of after your exit. I made the mistake, when selling one of my companies, of not doing the homework and contract negotiations necessary to look after the very people who had helped to make the company successful. I was so focused on the exit, that I didn't take the time to understand that the new company was going to have a different approach from mine, including wanting to consolidate the operations. Suddenly, many very talented and loyal people who had been with me from the beginning found themselves out of work. It was heartbreaking.

As appealing as exit strategies can sound to entrepreneurs who are just starting out and who are facing the toughest phase of their business, it is essential to remember that few businesses should be started with the sole purpose of selling. Exiting through cash flow should be every entrepreneur's dream. This means that your company is profitable and generates enough cash to pay its shareholders (in this case, you) a distribution of cash, sometimes referred to as a dividend. So if your company was successful enough to generate $100,000 in profit every month after taxes, and you own 80 percent, you earn $80,000 per month—for the rest of your life!

I highly recommend that you set up your business from the very first day with the idea that you are going to stay with it for the rest of your life. And before you consider leaving, ask yourself first if there is a way to reinvent yourself within the company.

When I was fund-raising for ViSalus, I met with Brian McLoughlin, a venture capitalist from Global Retail Partners in Los Angeles. We were discussing what the term sheet would look like if Global Retail Partners decided to put money into ViSalus and buy some of our personal shares. During the conversation he asked me, "If you get all this money, what are you going to do next?"

I said, "I'm going to build ViSalus."

Brian smiled. That's the commitment every venture capitalist is looking for. He said, "Good, because the entrepreneurs who are the most successful are the ones who stick with their businesses." For example, the two founders of Google, Larry Page and Sergey Brin, brought in Eric Schmidt after a painstaking search for a CEO, and picked the right guy to replace them in the duties they weren't right for. Eric helped take Google from less than $100 million to more than $200 billion in value. In short, Google made a great choice.

I took Brian's advice, stuck with ViSalus, and turned the company around, taking the company from $600,000 a month to over $12,000,000 in fifteen months. April 27, 2011, ViSalus received the Turn Around award from Direct Selling News. In 2012 ViSalus did over $600 million in sales. I am glad I stuck with it.

Now, if you have considered the alternatives and still come to the conclusion that it is time to exit your company, it's essential that you make sure your business is in good financial order.

In one acquisition I was considering, I pulled out because the company I was seeking to buy was not in financial order. I lost confidence in the business and retracted my offer during due diligence. This cost both parties lots of money, but for me, it wasn't worth the potential liabilities. Now when I advise entrepreneurs setting up a company, I tell them to follow all the requirements necessary to take it public eventually. Maybe one day they will take it public, or maybe one day a public company will want to buy their company. Either way, if your house is not in order, people will not want to buy it, especially not at a premium.

It is essential that you keep solid accounts of everything and have maintained good records of business matters, taxes, permits, and the like. Unfortunately, not everyone does this. I have seen countless entrepreneurs who would like to sell their businesses, but they are completely unable to produce tax records or payroll information for a year or two prior, or they are unable to answer even basic questions about their accounting procedures. This is unacceptable. It does not position you well for continued prosperity after the handover, and it certainly does not make the business appealing to potential buyers, because there may be substantial liabilities that aren't disclosed. This lack of organization will cost you far more time and money down the road when a buyer pulls out or offers to buy you at a discounted value. You have to make sure that every single aspect of your business is ready to be audited. In fact, most professional investors will require audited financials.

Believe me, I understand that when a company is first launched, the owner often does not have the time, knowledge, or understanding of some of these areas to be able to keep solid records on them all. I know I didn't at first, and that's understandable—it can be incredibly overwhelming. But at some point that has to change. If loose management becomes the established pattern for the company, any buyer is going to be leery of what else has been mismanaged. The most important hire for most entrepreneurs is their CFO, because the CFO's role is to enforce financial discipline and make sure the business model is being followed. This is one of the most important—and expensive—lessons I have learned in my career: hire a great CFO!

The next thing to consider is who will be taking over for you. This is especially important if you plan to maintain ownership of the company, because your ability to retire will depend on that person's ability to keep the business profitable.

You will want to make sure that you choose someone who is intimately familiar with your business. This often means hiring from inside the company, though not always. This is usually why in family businesses, the retiring parent will hand over control to a child. The reason isn't just nepotism. In many cases, the children have grown up around the company. They've watched the operations for decades, they know the employees by name, and they've heard business discussions around the dinner table since elementary school. That kind of deeply ingrained knowledge and understanding also leads to a sense of loyalty to the business. No one wants to be the person who undid Mom's life work or ran Grandpa's company into the ground. They take their business personally.

Don't let emotion or feelings of obligation crowd your thinking. You want to make sure that whomever you choose truly "gets" not only the product and marketplace of your business but also the culture of your company. You will never be able to replicate yourself perfectly, but you will want to choose someone with similar beliefs, philosophies, priorities, and principles, which is why a detailed understanding of how your company does business is so important.

Large corporations often hire new CEOs from other companies but usually from the same industry. When someone new is brought in from outside the company to assume the helm, the CEO's offerings are always supplemented by the insider knowledge from others, but he or she must thoroughly understand your company.

No matter what your long-term plan is, start engaging with prospective strategic partners early on. Use some of their services in your own company, and reach out to them with partnership ideas; this builds relationships and trust. It also enables you to learn how the other company works and lets you understand the entire landscape of the industry in a better way. SkyPipeline had a working relationship with NextWeb before we merged, which was helpful because, even as competitors, we had a mutual respect for each other. They admired our sales and marketing, and we admired their operational capacities. When we joined forces a year later, the transition was much smoother because that relationship was already in place. The same was true when we sold Path Connect to Solution X.

Don't make the mistake of putting on an overly aggressive front when meeting with your competitors. You should be a strong representative of your company, but don't overdo it in the hopes of impressing or intimidating them. I did that very thing in a meeting once, and it drove my small local competitor into the arms of a much bigger competitor. Their resulting merger hurt us a great deal. I will never forget the dinner I had with the owner of my number one competitor at SkyPipeline. He was open to a merger, and I jumped right in about how I was going to launch a marketing campaign to go after every one of his customers if he didn't do a deal with me. At the end of the meeting, our COO, Mark Ozur, pulled me aside and said, "I can't believe you. You need to learn how to build rapport and not be so competitive." He was right.

I should point out, though, that the exit scenario is not always a rosy one. Remember that you are still largely beholden to your investors and their expectations. I know of entrepreneurs who have had their investors' money tied up for eight or nine years without any returns, which obviously leaves the investors less than happy. In situations like that, the CEO is sometimes given the ultimatum of getting returns quickly or stepping down to make way for someone who can get the job done.

If you are in the position in which you have not yet made good on your investment promises, you should not consider leaving until you have or until you are forced out. It all goes back to some of those most fundamental lessons in business: you must be a good guardian of your investors' money.

As you make the decision about exiting, look back over your career to consider what you've built and what kind of legacy you are leaving behind. Are you satisfied with all you have done in the company you've created? The jobs you've provided? The contribution you've made to your community? The charitable works to which you've contributed? What about the satisfied customers for whom you've provided a quality product or a needed service? How about changes you've brought to the industry or advancements you've helped champion? In short, can you evaluate your efforts, understanding that there will always be growing pains and a learning curve, and say with peace, "I did my best"?

Imagine the gratification of a CEO or a founder of a company like Phil Knight, seeing his Nike products on people's feet as they walk down the street. Most consumers couldn't pick Phil Knight out of a crowd or sitting at a restaurant, but people do know that they love his shoes. He created value in our society. He created something remarkable and greater than himself. Warren Buffett remarked in an interview that he likes to buy companies that really contribute to society in some way. He likes to see the contribution. If he finds himself consuming the product, then he's looking at a good company to buy.

I've bought and sold three companies and I have no regrets because the experience taught me a very good lesson: if you don't have to start all over again—don't. When I left SkyPipeline I had to find a new team, test new marketing ideas, persuade new investors; it felt like starting from scratch without the family I was comfortable working with. Sure I had more money, but I realized that my true wealth wasn't in my bank account; it was in the team I had been cultivating and developing for years. As a result I swore I'd never lose a team like that again.

The truth is that some entrepreneurs never quite see the opportunity beyond where they are today. They turn their efforts into a glorified job, just like what they had before they left the corporate world to try things on their own. They have created their own Death Cycle in which they are forced to show up and deal with a management structure that is ineffective and unmotivated employees who are not right for the job. To me, this is about the most disappointing result of an entrepreneurial effort. Don't allow yourself to slip into that rut.

When Blyth bought ViSalus, we made a dozen millionaires on the spot, and laid the foundation for many more to cross that threshold over the next several years. Just knowing that a company I helped to grow could so drastically change those lives was an incredible reward. That's always been one of my dreams—to build businesses that support families, create value, and make positive changes of some sort in people's lives. I build companies with an eye toward contributing to the end user, the customer. And when you do that, you create a lot of value, and make a lot of money.

I sat down with the managing partners from the hedge fund Del Mar Assets the other day, and they asked me what other investments I had going besides ViSalus. I briefly explained the ten or so companies I had active investments in.

One of the partners said, "We'd like to invest in your next deal. How do we put some of our capital in your companies?" And I said, "You can't. I don't need money. I don't have an exit, so I don't give up equity."

Ultimately, your goal is to be able to say the same.

# 19

## TOLD U SO

---

In 2011, I was in New York celebrating the recent launch of my book, when I suddenly saw the Facebook app on my phone go berserk with thousands of inbound friend requests. I checked my e-mail to see if some sort of news had hit, and it turned out that Yahoo.com had put my picture with the title "From Gang Member to CEO" front and center on its homepage for millions of people to see.

At first I was excited that my book was getting such phenomenal PR and that my story was getting out there; being a writer was something I'd dreamed about since I was a kid in juvenile hall. Later that night, when I got back to my computer, I logged into the Yahoo homepage and saw over four thousand comments on the article. "I finally made it," I thought to myself. I was in awe, like a little kid who had just gotten his first trophy. I started reading the comments, scrolling down until one in particular puzzled me because it had been "liked" over eight hundred times. I paused on it. It was a teacher who appeared to be defending me.

I thought, "Who is this, and why are they defending me?" What I read next shifted my feeling of awe to a cringe in my stomach.

More people defending me. Then another person posting something cheering me up, and then another person claiming they were willing to go to war for me—all connected to the very comment that had started a comment war over me. There it was—thousands of people passionately loving and hating me right there on the Yahoo.com homepage. I paused and asked myself, "Is this what I really wanted?" To be loved, yes. But to be hated? No.

I was being criticized because I didn't follow an academic path, because I've been in trouble with the law, because I have tattoos, because I'm white and I listen to rap. Then there were the speculators who said that I was only successful because I'm involved in a scam. Or because I'm tall. Or because I somehow cheated the system or because the system had somehow cheated them.

Then there was a group who knew *exactly* why I was successful: because I was a fraud. They knew for a fact that I made my whole story up; it was all a lie. I'm really an underground criminal or a secret government project. Or my stepfather gave me all the money and I took credit for his work.

Then there were the ones who were just damn funny. "I didn't know New Kids On The Block was a gang" or "Is that the ShamWow guy?"

As I slogged through the comments, reading the variety of posts from total strangers who decided they were going to take shots at me and seeing my fans and friends responding with counterattacks, the feeling in my stomach turned from pain to anger. The job of the artist is to educate the critic, and I was going to educate all these haters not by commenting, but by action; not by words, but by results.

My whole life I have tried to prove my worth—that I wasn't just some dyslexic special education kid from a poor family who made poor decisions. I wasn't going to let these haters hold me down.

Later, I called one of my mentors, legendary Coach Dale Brown. I said, "Coach, I'm being absolutely torn apart right now, publically, everywhere. What should I do?"

Dale raised his voice and charged at me over the phone, like I was one of his basketball players sulking in the locker room. He said, "Ryan, just make sure they get your damn name right."

I took Coach's advice, and like he implied, I had to grow a thick skin. So what, I got roasted by a bunch of anonymous cowards on Yahoo.com. I also got thousands of followers. The opposite of love isn't hate—it's indifference. Love and hate are closely connected. So love me or hate me—just get my damn name right.

As an entrepreneur you're going to lose friends—probably most of the people you grew up with. And you might even lose family like I have because you've decided to challenge the belief systems that these people have about you—and more importantly about themselves—that they've clung to for the majority of their mediocre lives. And if you're a good entrepreneur, your belief in yourself will be so strong that those who don't understand it won't understand you. People fear what they don't understand. Are you ready for that? Being a CEO is the loneliest job on the planet and sometimes your only friend is "Told U So."

As Drake said, "I started off local but thanks to all the haters, I know G4 pilots on a first-name basis."

# EPILOGUE: ON TO THE NEXT ONE

A few years ago, I was driving down a street in Montreal, having just come from breakfast at a little French-Canadian café, when I stopped at a red light and checked my BlackBerry. I was relishing the incredible travel opportunities and sudden fame my work had brought me. There were a few e-mails from people I knew who had seen my recent appearance on the Donny Deutsch show and were writing to congratulate me—and then I opened a message that threw me for a loop. It was very short, saying simply, "I am proud of you. You should know that your grandmother is very ill."

Staring at that tiny screen, I was mystified. It didn't seem to be from any of my siblings or my mom. Was it some distant relative? Who would be writing me something like that? And then I scrolled down and my eyes fell on the most unbelievable word in the signature: "Dad." My dad had sent me an e-mail. The man who had been gone from my life without a trace for nearly fifteen years—no Christmas cards or calls on my birthday or child support checks to my mom—just a complete void from the day he'd disappeared. And now he was writing to congratulate me.

I pulled my car over as a torrent of emotions swept over me. I had waited more than half my life for this moment, to reconnect with him, and now the opportunity was sitting in the palm of my hand. During the intervening years I had passed through all the stages of hurt and anger I'd felt toward him—not just for what he had done to my mom and to me, but for what he had done to ruin himself and the life he had built. As time passed, I had finally been able to let go of all of that, and I wanted tell him that I forgave him and loved him, but I'd never known how to reach him. Until now.

Less than one minute after his message arrived, I was typing out a response that was almost fifteen years in the making. I told him that I owed some of my success to the character traits he'd taught me as a child, especially the work ethic and how to channel ambition. I told him I wanted him to sleep peacefully at night knowing that I was grateful for the lessons he had given me. And I told him that although I would never forget what he'd done to my mom and me, he would always be my father, and I'd always be his son.

After that day, I began to write the first half of my life story, called *Faith of the Dots.* The title was inspired by a speech Steve Jobs gave at Stanford University about how our lives are a series of unrelated events until we connect them.

For *Faith of the Dots,* I started with a list of two hundred of my most vivid memories as a mnemonic device. As the chapters accumulated, I realized that the return of my father was the event that would enable me to become a father myself and embrace fatherhood with a sense of responsibility. I wouldn't repeat the vicious cycle of abuse. I wanted to forgive the man who had been so evil to me and my family, and to remove the emotional scar tissue as well as the behavioral patterns he burned into me. Most important, I wanted my son, Ryan Reagan Blair, to begin his dots unbound by his father's—and his grandfather's—limitations. I wanted him to start his life free of the ghosts that haunt our family's past and to be proud of his name, because I hadn't been.

But somehow I never felt a sense of completion from the reconciliation with my father. There was still a piece missing.

This year, after my stepfather died of cancer and as I was dealing with the loss day after day, I realized that I had never closed the wound from the disappearance of my biological father, not even after he contacted me that day in Montreal. I was still thinking of myself as someone who had no father.

The truth is I'd had a father all along, but I never made the connection that Bob was my real dad because I got him when I was already seventeen years old. I'd come to live with him when I was no longer innocent. Even though it hadn't occurred to me, Bob always knew he was my real father. He knew that he'd raised me and that someday I'd come around to realizing it. He knew that although I'd looked like a man when he met me, with gang tattoos and battle scars, I was still a thirteen-year-old boy on the inside. I had no self-confidence and a ton of negative internal programming to overcome.

My stepfather set about reprogramming me. He dared me to dream, and he believed in me until the day I could believe in myself. Bob, true to form, lived elegantly and he died elegantly, on top of his game. When we laid him to rest, he gave me something more valuable than any of his other gifts: he gave me closure on a wound I could never have healed on my own, but opened up one that almost sent me right back to where I started.

As I mentioned in Honor Your Deals, I made a commitment to Bob on his deathbed, I promised him that after he passed, I'd take care of my mother. At the time I didn't know what that promise meant. Or how it would be put to the test.

Exactly ninety days after we lost my stepfather, I woke one morning with a clear mind. I'd finally caught my breath. It was March 2011, and this book was going into production; the publisher was printing our first set of copies to be released to a select list of celebrities, friends, and influencers. On my way back from a trip to Miami where I had been partying like a rock star (literally, with rock stars) I stopped at our ViSalus headquarters in Michigan to meet the 50 some new employees we'd hired to handle my company's sudden growth.

The irony is that while my personal life had hit bottom in the wake of my stepfather's death, everything else—my career as an author, fatherhood, and our company's financial goals—all came into focus. One event summed up the extremes going on in my life at the time: delivering a eulogy to several hundred friends and family members at the funeral of the man who taught me everything about finance, as I was making the biggest financial gains of my lifetime.

In the midst of this, my family was simultaneously coming together and falling apart. We rallied around my mother as she went into a rapid downward spiral caused by a broken heart, and we knew that no matter how overwhelming our grief was, it was nothing compared to hers. She'd lost her soul mate.

Just as I landed in Michigan I got word from my sister and brother in law. My mother had fallen down a flight of stairs, and had been found lying with a cracked skull on the marble floor in the foyer, twelve hours later.

I rushed back to Los Angeles.

My mother is a beautiful woman, slender and fair-haired. She used to get pegged for Farrah Fawcett when the actress was in her heyday. And my mother knew she was gorgeous; she used to make us crazy spending three hours in the bathroom getting ready when we were kids. I walked into the hospital and there she was; nothing could have prepared me for the sight. Her head was shaved, and all her blond curls were gone. Half of her skull had been removed and she had a row of staples and stitches that spanned from her forehead to the back of her neck up where they'd performed a marathon surgery, 10 hours long. There were tubes and wires coming in and out of her nose and throat. The doctor told me point blank that my mom had a 1 percent change of coming out of the coma; the brain damage was severe. And even less than 1 percent chance, if she did come back, of ever having a life worth living.

My mother is the strongest woman I've ever known. She's my hero. She taught me to love and to be positive no matter how bad our situation seemed. Most important my mother always taught me that when you fall down, you get back up, and you stand strong. When I was a kid and I'd hurt myself, my mother would make me stand up. She'd say, be a man. You're stronger than that. This is a woman who worked a job at a local deli making minimum wage to support her family. I remember her stepping in front of my father and taking beating after beating so that I wouldn't have to. She had no resources to provide for us, but she still sacrificed herself to make sure we had a chance. I remember visiting her in hospital after my father gave her a near death beating and when she finally stood up to his evil rage with the courage of a woman without fear of life and death, and her coming to see me in jail when I'd started making bad decisions of my own. It broke her heart because I wasn't living up to the potential she told me I had.

If it weren't for her example of strength, I wouldn't be here now and, I wouldn't be able to go on now. After I got the news of my mother's condition, I immediately reached out to my ViSalus family via my Facebook page and asked for their prayers and support while my mother was having brain surgery and I was on a five-hour flight to see her. The longest five hours of my life. I sat there crying, thinking about all the times we had together, all the times we might not have together, thinking my son will never know his dad's parents, and that I could have been a better son myself. I mourned the fact that my poor mother had been lying on that floor for twelve hours without help as she slipped away, not into the next world, but to a middle world where she couldn't experience heaven on earth, or beyond it. I prayed for a miracle.

I had a hard time asking for the help of the thousands of people in my network, because I didn't want pity. I wanted their energy, I wanted God to hear, and I wanted my mother to feel 10,000 prayers, because it was all I could do. I was helpless and just as my mother taught me when "you're helpless, get on your knees and pray." And I would pray to God every day.

## VIII-IV-XI

My mother had been on life support since March 29, 2011. And my heart was broken every single day. The days when I could see her it would break my heart because I couldn't do anything to end her suffering, and the days when I could not see her I felt like she was laying there wondering why I hadn't come by in so long. I was torn between my ambition and my love for my mother.

She wouldn't have wanted it that way, but since she didn't have a living will, we weren't able to end her suffering as she would have wished. On October 22, 2012, the two-year anniversary of my stepfather's unexpected death, our family went to court and was granted permission to honor my mother's wishes and take her off life support.

From the day she fell down that flight of stairs I would pray to God that he grant her a miracle or mercy. Over the next eighteen months my heart began to grow cold. I couldn't give myself to anyone but my mother and my son, who both needed me desperately.

I have been through every emotion you can imagine—all the ups and downs—as I've had to learn how to deal with my mother's suffering while I was doing everything but suffering, at least on the outside. This struggle taught me to compartmentalize—to apply extreme focus toward difficult and traumatic events, and then close the compartment and move on to the next one. The one compartment I couldn't open was to let myself truly love another woman. It was too dangerous and complicated.

After my mom got injured, I felt alone and misunderstood. I hit an all-time low. I was so angry. I was still mourning the loss of my stepfather, I wasn't sure where my company and career were going next, and the only thing I was certain about was that the hardcover edition of this book was coming out on August 4. I was nervous it would be a failure. I was exposing a lot about myself and I was worried people would judge me (and they did). Because my mother had just had her fall, and because I had a new perspective on life, I started to reflect, and then rewrote the book for the hundredth time to incorporate my traumatic loss and new point of view. One day at her bedside I decided right then and there that it would become a *New York Times* bestseller in honor of my mother and that I would stop at nothing to make that dream a reality. I vividly recall leaning over and whispering in her ear that I was going to put my heart and soul into writing it, and I would do my absolute best to not allow the grief and pain of my loss to ruin my chance of fulfilling my dream of telling her story. I told her it was our dream, and that I knew she wouldn't want me to fail because of her fall. I once again acted like I had nothing to lose. I was on a mission to make my mother proud.

The day I thought I would be looking forward to the most—getting my first book published—finally came on August 4, 2011. It would also be the day my family went to court to get custodianship of my mother and the day I would find out my son had autism. The date 8-4-11 is tattooed on my forearm for that very reason. It represents the duality of my life. It's the day I love and understand the most.

August 4, 2011, taught me that life is about the journey, not the destination. Like most people, I thought if I were rich I'd be happy. Because my early years were deprived, I craved success, and up until 8-4-11 my only source of fuel was the taste of success. Now my fuel comes from a spiritual source.

October 22, 2012, will also be a day I remember for the rest of my life. It was the day the courts granted my mom the mercy I had been praying for. On that day I went to visit my mom in the hospital to tell her that I would take her home and remove her from life support within a few days. I told her that if she wanted to live she was going to have to show it. I explained to her that I would have to remove her feeding tube and that she would starve to death without it. I told her that I would be by her side and that ending her life would break mine, but that I would do it as she wished. I told her that it would be my honor and I wished she could just wake up and tell me what she wanted so that I knew for sure it was the right decision.

My sister and I would visit her while she was in a coma and explain to her what our next steps were. Ten days after the court order, I visited my mom, and her eyes were wide open. This wasn't abnormal. My mom's eyes were often open; they just never made a connection with you. This day when I entered her hospital room, she was different. I could sense it. I said, "Mom, blink your eyes: once for yes, twice for no." She lay there with here blue eyes staring at me, her hair gray, a large part of her skull removed near her temple, face pale, and, to my amazement, she did it.

She blinked once for yes and twice for no. Then I said, "Mom?" almost to ask the question, "Are you there?" She turned her head and smiled and blinked once for yes.

I was floored. A surge of joy ran through me. I rushed to her bedside, gently took her head in my hands, and looked deeply in her eyes. Tears streamed down my face and splashed onto hers. Thinking this might be the only chance I had to know whether she wanted to live or die, the first question I asked her was, "Mom, do you want to live or die?" She looked at me deeply, smiled and said with a faint whisper, "Live."

I have never felt a greater joy in my life and have never been more grateful to God for teaching me that miracles do happen.

My mother started making great progress from that day forward. She began talking again, moving her arms and legs, and within days of waking up was in physical rehab. I have my mother back, and we have hope that she will make a full recovery.

From this journey I now believe that all pain in life is delivered to make you stronger—a battle test from God. The greater the test, the greater the strength you'll derive from it. My belief is that God likes to test his soldiers. I believe in the power of prayer and I am eternally grateful to everyone who prayed for my family and my mom's recovery.

I've shared this profoundly personal story with you because I hope you embrace every battle test with a similar philosophy. This is the skill you'll have to develop for dealing with each blow life deals you on your way to becoming someone you're proud of, because no matter how successful you are, you only live once—and you have everything to gain.

# SUPPORT THE BOOK!

If you liked the book, tweet the following: Loved@RyanBlair's book Nothing to Lose.

Become a fan: www.facebook.com/ryanblair.fans.

Contact me at ryan@nothingtolose.com.

For behind the scenes footage of the writing of this book, interviews, lifestyle and business tips, subscribe to my private video vault at www.nothingtolose.com.

And for additional resources for students and educators based on the material in this book, please visit www.nothingtolose.com/resources.

# ACKNOWLEDGMENTS

There are many people in my life whom I want to thank. Everything I have learned, I have learned from someone. I first want to thank God for giving me the faith necessary to overcome many obstacles. And second, I thank my entire family because they are the people who kept me from the edge of many cliffs. Kasie Head for giving me the greatest gift I have ever known, my son, Ryan Reagan Blair. My mother, Erla Hunt, and my late stepfather Robert Hunt, for leading me out of adversity and being role models. Thank you, Stephanie Gager, the best big sister a little brother could have. My grandmother Wini, for instilling in me spirituality and teaching me unconditional love.

I also want to thank the people most responsible for making this book a reality; first, my writing partner Shannon Constantine Logan for helping me put my stories and philosophies on paper. Don Yaeger, thank you for having the confidence in me to pass up many projects to make this book happen. I'd also like to acknowledge Dave Moldawer and Kirby Kim of William Morris Endeavor; Dave for believing in me enough to publish me, and Kirby for being a good agent; as well as Emily Angell, Bria L. Sandford, Adrian Zackheim, and the sales and marketing team at Portfolio/Penguin. Coach Dale Brown, I appreciate you for your mentorship and for introducing me to Don and Coach John Wooden, two people who have added indescribable value to my life. Daniel Decker, Stephanie Jones, Andrew Sandler, Brian Stafford, Tiffany Brooks, Erica Jennings, Matt Sinnreich, Jade Charles, John Laun, Karl Stedman, Joe Perez, Michelle Gignon, Emily Schatz, and Hasina Deary. Many thanks to Sam ben-Avraham and the Atrium team for styling me on countless occasions.

Many thanks to my partners in ViSalus—Todd Goergen, Nick Sarnicola, and Blake Mallen—thank you for bringing me on as a partner and for companies. You guys are the most talented and dedicated people I've ever worked with. I also want to thank the ViSalus Employees & Executive team, ROPART Asset Management, and the Blyth team. I'd like to acknowledge the *Nothing to Lose* book launch team, Daniel Decker; Ashley Huebner; Bryan Stafford; Andrew Sandler; Vertical KI; Jace Perry; Fortier PR; Julian Chavez; Andy Jenkins; Allison McLean; and Jacquelynn Burke. Also, Stuart Johnson and the teams at Video Plus, *Success Magazine*, and *Direct Selling News*.

Last, I want to thank every person who ever invested in my ventures; it is because of your willingness to take a risk that the entrepreneurial world goes round.

# SPECIAL ACKNOWLEDGMENTS

To the ViSalus leaders, without your sacrifice and hard work, none of this could happen; Nick and Ashley Sarnicola; Jason O'Toole and Jennifer Creamer; Mike and Lavon Craig; Kyle Pacetti; Tony and Rhonda Lucero; Rachel and Josh Jackson; Jeremy Gilchrist; Bonzi Saycosie and Shelly Goschka; Bryan and Brandi Bellville; Scott and Jenny Lynn-Travis; Tim and Holley Kirkland; Kevin and Stephanie Merriweather; Chad and Joni Robbins; Aaron Fortner; Matt and Leigh Ward; Freddy and Catherine Melero; Susan Pacetti; Dale Peake and Robyn Peake; Sarah and Barry Midthun; Tara Wilson; Matthew Britt and Mia St-Aubin; Tanis MacDonald and Lorne Humenny; R.J. and Samantha Barros; Scott and Shana Falany; Luke and Deb Pennucci; Todd and Christina Perry; Alan and Heather Guzzino; Cedrick Harris; Tina and Ken Hockmuth; Tim Sharif; Matt and Johnna Parr; Ryan and Kristen Johnson; Lori Petrilli; Sylvain Laplante and Lori Parent; Charles Marion; Frank Varon; Kevin Latmore; and the entire ViSalus community for believing in a vision greater than all of us.

# INDEX